The Complete Book of
Vegetarian
Barbecuing

The Complete Book of
Vegetarian
Barbecuing

Over 150 Delicious Recipes plus
tips and techniques

Susann Geiskopf-Hadler

APPLE

Text © 2005 by Susann Geiskopf-Hadler

First published in the UK in 2005 by
Apple Press
112-116a Western Road
Hove BN3 1DD
www.apple-press.com

08 07 06 05 04 1 2 3 4 5

ISBN 1-84543-016-6

Library of Congress Cataloging-in-Publication Data available

Cover design by Mary Ann Smith
Book design by Yee Design

Printed and bound in China

Dedication

I dedicate this book to Guy Hadler, my barbecue-master, sous-chef, and loving husband.

Acknowledgments

I'd like to thank some of my regular diners, those taste-testers who consistently come over for dinner to prep the meal with me, set the table, and then even clean up and help load the dishwasher. Bunnie Day, Joseph Angello, Dennis Newhall, Yvonne Shanks, Candy and Al Holland, Cecelia and Michael Marsden – your help was invaluable. You all demanded that I 'take a break' to enjoy a glass of wine, assuring me that you were now well fed. I also want to thank all of you not mentioned here by name for making the time to pop over for a spontaneous meal.

I thank my husband, Guy Hadler, for letting me sleep in on Sunday mornings while he went to the farmers' market to purchase many of the fresh ingredients I used to prepare the delicious recipes in this book. Thank you also for tending to the vegetable and herb gardens as I sat in front of the computer. And your mastery of the barbecue is also to be commended.

Table of Contents

8   Introduction ✻ A World of Delight

10   Chapter 1 ✎ Barbecuing Tools, Terms, and Techniques

20   Chapter 2 ☞ Seasoning Sauces and Marinades

34   Chapter 3 ☀ Salsas, Chutneys, and Dipping Sauces

54   Chapter 4 ✺ Hors d'Oeuvres, Dips, and Spreads

74   Chapter 5 ♤ Salads and Side Dishes

102   Chapter 6 ✤ Pizza and *en Papillote* Entrées

124   Chapter 7 ✿ Pasta, Grain, and Polenta Dishes

154   Chapter 8 ◌ Skewered Entrées

170   Chapter 9 ✾ Fajitas, Tacos, Burritos, and Quesadillas

188   Chapter 10 ✸ Wraps, Sandwiches, and Burgers

204   Chapter 11 ❂ Barbecued Desserts

214   Glossary of Speciality Ingredients

       Index

Introduction
A World of Delight

IF YOUR CONCEPT OF VEGETARIAN BARBECUING IS LIMITED TO veggie kebabs and corn on the cob, a whole world of culinary delight awaits you here. Never again will you have to stand by while your meat-eating friends rave about how easy and fun it is to barbecue delicious meals outdoors or in. In fact, once you start serving meals from *The Complete Book of Vegetarian Barbecuing*, they'll be begging you for the recipes!

That's because 'complete' isn't in the title by accident. From appetizers through delicious desserts hot off the barbecue, you'll find more than 150 phenomenal recipes for salads, light and hearty main dishes, dips, sauces, salsas, side dishes, sandwiches, and even pizza.

This book embraces the diversity of flavours and textures that can be created by cooking vegetables and fruits on the barbecue. The flavours, shapes, colours, and textures found in the vegetable kingdom offer endless possibilities when paired with creative seasonings, grains, breads, pastas, and cheeses. And you'll find delicious recipes from around the world to broaden your barbecuing horizons.

Barbecuing is a fast and easy and simple to master. You can use a gas barbecue, a charcoal barbecue, or an indoor electric or stove-top barbecue. I prefer an outdoor gas barbecue for its convenience. It heats up fast, offers an even barbecuing temperature, ensures consistent cooking times, and is easy to clean. You can even add smoky flavour by putting wood chips on the hot barbecue bed. But I've included directions for every barbecue type in these recipes to guarantee success no matter what you're using.

Luckily for all of us who love the ease and delicious flavours of barbecued food, barbecuing is no longer a seasonal occupation. Summertime is synonymous with firing up the gas or charcoal barbecue when the long, warm nights invite us to dine alfresco. But the cooler months are also an ideal time of the year to cook on the outdoor barbecue, since the heat that emanates from the barbecue provides warmth on a cool night. Additionally, many kitchens are now equipped with built-in barbecues or electric barbecuing appliances, turning barbecuing into a year-round cooking option.

Outdoor barbecuing is not just easy, it's entertaining. The aroma in the open air excites the taste buds for the culinary pleasures to come. Because barbecuing tends to be more casual than indoor food preparation, dining is more informal, giving you and your family or guests license to laugh and linger. So get ready to linger over the luscious array of recipes on these pages, as you plan the first of many enticing meals to come.

CHAPTER 1
Barbecuing Tools, Terms, and Techniques

In order to be at ease with any food preparation, you have to be at ease with the tools and techniques involved. This chapter covers the essential types of barbecuing equipment you'll need to prepare the recipes in this book, the fundamental techniques for barbecuing, and basic cooking terms, along with some simple techniques for preparing ingredients.

Choosing an Outdoor Barbecue

A vast assortment of barbecues – both charcoal and gas – are available for outdoor barbecuing. Indoor electric barbecues may also be used to barbecue some of the recipes in this book; I'll talk about indoor electric barbecues on page 15. Consider how many people you usually cook for to help you decide what size barbecue to purchase. The biggest decision for outdoor barbecuing, however, is choosing between a charcoal or gas grill.

There are some pros and cons for each type. Charcoal barbecues traditionally burn a bit hotter than many gas barbecues, impart a smoke flavour, make it easier to add wood chips to the coals, and are less expensive to purchase than their gas counterparts. However, they take longer to start and heat up than gas barbecues, they require constant attention, they are messy because of ash and charcoal debris, and their temperatures are harder to control.

Gas barbecues are convenient, and the newer models get as hot as charcoal barbecues. Most start with the push of a button, they heat up quickly, you control the heat with the turn of a knob, and they have built-in temperature gauges. Some even come with built-in smoker boxes, or you can add a smoker box to achieve a similar effect to adding wood chips to a charcoal grill. Some gas barbecues also come with side burners that allow you to cook pasta or grains or to prepare a sauce while you are barbecuing the entrée. This feature allows you to stay at the barbecue, rather then go between the barbecue and the stovetop.

So where is the downside to gas, you ask? Gas barbecues are more expensive to purchase, and many barbecue aficionados consider 'true' barbecuing to be cooking over charcoal or wood coals. Investigate the options, read the brochures, and talk with friends – or better yet, try out their barbecues! – and then decide which type of barbecue is right for you.

A gas barbecue is fueled by propane, so you have to remember to refill the propane tank or to keep a spare one on hand. If you are designing an outdoor kitchen, you can have the gas line plumbed directly to your propane line for an endless supply of fuel.

If you choose a charcoal grill, consider natural lump charcoal rather than charcoal briquettes, which contain large quantities of chemical lighter fluid, these barbecue food with a harsh, acrid flavour. Lump charcoal is available in different hardwoods, such as alder, hickory, and mesquite. It starts quicker, burns hotter, and smells better than briquettes. You will need only about half as much lump charcoal as you would briquettes to achieve the desired temperature.

Some specific tools are necessary no matter what type of barbecue you choose; others are only necessary for a charcoal grill. Many of these tools are available only in stores that specialize in barbecuing supplies; others can be found wherever you shop for kitchen tools.

Tools for the Barbecue

These tools will make your barbecuing easy and fun. Here's what you'll need:

- A chimney starter is a chemical-free way to ignite lump charcoal or briquettes. This large, upright, hollow, metal cylinder with a wire partition in the centre will allow you to ignite coals in minutes. Look for a chimney starter capable of holding 6 litres of charcoal.

- A disposable can or shallow aluminum tray is useful for soaking wood chips.

- A smoker box is used for placing wood chips on the gas grill.

- A long-handled, hand-held garden hoe is handy for raking hot charcoal into an even layer on the grill.

- A stiff wire brush is invaluable for cleaning the grill.

- Long-handled tongs and spatulas are perfect for turning and then removing barbecued food when it's done.

- Insulated mitts are essential for removing hot ingredients from the barbecue and the hot barbecue rack or barbecue basket.

- Long-handled, natural-bristle basting brushes are handy to brush marinades on foods as they grill. Avoid nylon basting brushes because the nylon will melt when basting hot food.

- Cooking parchment or heavy-duty aluminum foil is necessary for *en papillote* cooking.

- A baking stone to place directly on the barbecue is necessary for cooking pizza and *en papillote* preparations. You can find them in both round and square shapes to match your barbecue's design.

- Cooking bricks or tiles can be positioned to hold the ends of skewers to prevent them from burning or to place foods directly on top of the barbecue to prevent the bottom of foods from burning.

- Large, shallow glass dishes are indispensable to hold ingredients in a single layer while they marinate.

- An assortment of metal and bamboo skewers are necessary for skewered entrées.

- A kitchen timer, or maybe two – one for out by the barbecue and one for inside – because you may be going back and forth between the barbecue and the stovetop.

- A portable flat metal barbecue grate or barbecue basket will keep small vegetables from falling through the barbecue grates but allow the smoke and flames to pass through the holes.

- A hinged barbecue basket for holding delicate foods together as you barbecue them is very useful. This allows you to turn the food without it falling apart because it is securely locked in place inside the barbecue basket.

- Cutting boards, trays, and large platters are important to place the hot barbecued foods on as you transport them from the barbecue to the table.

Techniques for Outdoor Barbecuing

Barbecuing utilizes dry heat at high temperatures. The close contact with a hot flame quickly cooks foods and lends a characteristic barbecued flavour. There is a mystique surrounding barbecuing, but this cooking method has been around since the discovery of fire. Become familiar with the unique features of your particular barbecue, stay by it so the food is not overcooked, and you'll soon have mastered the fun and easy skill of barbecuing.

There are two distinct barbecuing methods – barbecuing and indirect barbecuing. Barbecuing cooks food directly over glowing coals or the flame from a gas barbecue. Food is cooked at a medium to high temperature in a matter of minutes. The barbecue will be hooded during the cooking time except when you open it to turn the food.

Traditionally, indirect barbecuing calls for the fire to be on one side of the barbecue while the food is cooked away from the flame, on the barbecue but over the unlit portion. Some recipes in this book call for a slightly different indirect barbecuing technique where you place a baking stone or bricks on the barbecue to turn it into a sort of outdoor convection oven with the heat circulating around the food as it cooks. With this indirect barbecuing method, the food is not turned as it cooks, and the temperature is a bit lower. The barbecue is kept covered during the recommended cooking time.

Preheating the Barbecue

Barbecue temperatures and cooking times are not as exact as when baking something in an oven. It is important, however, to preheat to the temperature range called for in a specific recipe.

To preheat a charcoal barbecue, use a chimney starter. Place a crumpled sheet of newspaper in the bottom of the chimney starter. Place the starter on the bottom grate of your grill. Place the lump charcoal (or briquettes) in the top of the starter, filling to the top. Light the newspaper. You will see a thick column of smoke as the paper burns and the charcoal begins to ignite. Allow the coals to become orange-red in colour – this will take about 15 to 25 minutes. Wearing barbecue mitts, dump the coals from the chimney starter into the bottom of the grill. Use a garden hoe to rake the coals into a single layer. Place the barbecuing grate on the grill. The coals will turn mostly to ash after about an hour. You can replenish them by raking the coals into a pile and placing unlit lump charcoal (or briquettes) on them. Leave the barbecue uncovered until the fresh charcoal lights.

To preheat a charcoal barbecue to high, light the coals and rake them over the bottom of the barbecue surface with the top and bottom vents wide open. Allow about 30 minutes to bring the coals to the correct temperature. This will give you a hot grill, about 260°C/gas mark 10+. Test this by holding your hand over the coals. If you can only keep it there for about 2 seconds, the barbecue is hot enough. You could also use a thermometer to measure the temperature.

To preheat the coals to medium-high, follow

the same procedure as described above, but rake the coals a bit thinner and allow them to burn for 5 to 10 minutes longer. You should be able to hold your hand over them for about 3 to 4 seconds, or use a thermometer to measure the temperature to read about 200°C/gas mark 6.

A medium barbecue is just a bit cooler than a medium-high grill, so allow the coals to burn a bit longer. You should be able to hold your hand over them for about 5 to 6 seconds, or use a thermometer to measure the temperature to read about 175°C/gas mark 4.

A medium-low barbecue is about 165°/gas mark 3, and a low barbecue temperature is about 150°C/gas mark 2. You will be able to hold your hand over the coals for about 8 to 10 seconds for a medium-low temperature or 10 to 12 seconds for a low temperature. Again, use a thermometer to check the temperature if you wish.

To preheat a gas barbecue to high, ignite the starter button on the barbecue and set the control knobs to high. This will bring the temperature to 260° to 290°C/gas mark 10+. The barbecue will take about 10 minutes to heat up.

To preheat a gas barbecue to medium-high, preheat the barbecue to high, and then turn the burners down to about 200°C/gas mark 6. Oddly enough, this will take about 15 minutes because you will need to allow the barbecue to cool a bit.

For a medium grill, preheat the barbecue to high, and then back the temperature off to about 175°C/gas mark 4. Allow about 18 to 20 minutes to reach the desired temperature. Medium-low, about 165°C/gas mark 3, and low, about

150°C/gas mark 2, will take a few more minutes to back off the higher initial temperature.

Best Barbecuing Techniques

Some special tips apply, regardless of what type of barbecue you use or the barbecue temperature you need. As with most tips, they are logical, but they are sometimes overlooked. Make sure *you* don't overlook them if you want to barbecue like a pro and enjoy the best, most flavourful food!

◉ Keep the barbecue clean. Fresh food will stick to left-over food that is on the barbecue from the last meal. Brush the barbecue grate after you have preheated the barbecue and after you have finished cooking. Use the edge of a metal spatula to scrape off large bits of food, and then thoroughly brush with a wire brush.

◉ Have everything you need prepped and ready at barbecue side before you start barbecuing.

◉ Make sure your barbecue tools are clean and beside the grill.

◉ Make sure the barbecue is sitting level and is stable.

◉ Barbecue in a well-ventilated, open area.

◉ Do not wear flowing or loose clothing. It is more likely to catch fire than snug-fitting attire.

◉ Preheat the barbecue to the correct temperature. Make sure you have enough charcoal or propane so you don't run out in the middle of barbecuing.

- Oil the grate just before placing food on top of it. Spray the grate or rub it with a paper towel that has been soaked with oil.

- Keep a spray bottle of water near the barbecue to put out minor flare-ups. Use water sparingly, as it can warp the barbecue and the flavour bars of a gas grill.

- Some foods will require basting as they cook. Keep your marinade and basting brush by the grill, ready to use as needed.

- Never place hot or warm coals from the barbecue in a rubbish bin! Allow coals to cool completely before disposing of them.

- Always turn off the gas barbecue when barbecuing is completed. It's best to turn the propane valve to the off position on the propane tank because many systems will let small amounts of propane leak out, which will drain the tank prematurely.

Indoor Barbecues

Indoor electric barbecues are in their own category of barbecuing equipment. They offer the quick preparation that barbecuing on a charcoal or gas barbecue does, but with the convenience of indoor cooking. For those who live in cold-winter areas, and for everyone who'd enjoy barbecuing no matter what the weather outside, this can be a real plus. Electric barbecues function like inverted barbecues, giving food grill marks as it cooks on the hot grate.

Electric barbecues are not replacements for their outdoor counterparts, but they do offer a year-round solution for quick and healthy barbecued meals. Most recipes that are cooked directly on the barbecue can be prepared on an indoor electric one with slightly different, but delicious, results.

There are different styles of portable indoor electric barbecues and grills available. The most common are two-sided grills, combination barbecues, and stovetop grill pans.

Two-sided grills have two grilling plates that are hinged. They open and close like a book so that they simultaneously contact the food on two opposite sides. They are well suited to cooking sliced vegetables and some of the burger recipes in this book. The food cooks fast because the heat source cooks on both sides simultaneously. These barbecues usually do not have a temperature control setting, so food cooks on only one heat setting, usually medium-high.

Combination barbecues are shallow, 3- to 6-cm-deep electric fry pans with evenly spaced grilling ridges. The pan heats up and the food cooks on the grilling ridges. These pans come in a round or rectangular shape with a lid. You can use them at the table or on a side bar to captivate your guests as you prepare the meal.

Another popular indoor barbecuing method is to use a grill pan on your gas stovetop burners. You can control the temperature by adjusting the stovetop knobs. Purchase a thick, heavy pan made of cast iron.

Techniques for Indoor Barbecuing

Some special tips apply to indoor barbecuing.

- Turn on the kitchen exhaust fan or set the grill up in a well-ventilated location.

- Oil the grill before placing food on top of it. Rub the grill surface with a paper towel that has been soaked with oil.

- Always turn off or unplug the grill when barbecuing is completed.

- Clean the grill between each use with warm soapy water, or, if the grill surface is dishwasher-safe, place it in the dishwasher after each use.

Basic Cooking Terms

Recipes are full of terminology, some of which can sound like a foreign language if you are not familiar with their meanings. I've listed the basic cooking terms that are used in this book here in alphabetical order for quick reference.

- **Al dente.** Italian phrase (literally meaning 'to the tooth') describing pasta that is tender but still a bit chewy.

- **Blanch.** To cook briefly in boiling water; frequently done to loosen the skin of a fruit or vegetable for easy peeling.

- **Blend.** To mix two or more ingredients until thoroughly combined.

- **Boil.** To cook in rapidly bubbling liquid.

- **Chiffonade.** French technique in which leafy herbs or other greens are stacked and rolled into a loose cylinder, then sliced crosswise into paper-thin shreds using a sharp knife.

- **Chill.** To place in the refrigerator for a designated time.

- **Chop, finely.** To cut into pieces about the size of a pea.

- **Chop, coarsely.** To cut into larger, irregular pieces.

- **Cool.** To remove from the heat and let stand at room temperature.

- **Dice.** To cut into cubes of roughly uniform size.

- **Dice, finely.** To cut into very small cubes of roughly uniform size.

- **Emulsified.** Referring to a combination of ingredients that has been vigorously whipped together, often using a wire whisk, until they are completely blended and slightly thickened.

- ***En papillote.*** Literally meaning 'in paper,' a French cooking method in which ingredients are baked in a tightly closed paper packet, producing a moist and aromatic dish. *The 'Pizza and en Papillote Entrées' chapter beginning on page 102 gives detailed instructions for packaging en Papillote entrées.*

- **Fork-tender.** Referring to vegetables that are easily pierced with a fork, but still firm enough to retain their shape.

- **Marinate.** To place food in seasoned liquid for a period of time, infusing it with the flavours of the marinade.

- **Mince.** To cut into tiny uniform pieces.

- **Mix.** To stir ingredients together until evenly distributed.

- **Pack, firmly.** To place an ingredient in a measuring cup or spoon and compress with your hand or a wooden spoon.
- **Pack, lightly.** To place an ingredient in a measuring cup or spoon without compressing.
- **Sauté.** To lightly brown ingredients in oil or other liquid.
- **Simmer.** To cook in gently bubbling liquid.
- **Steam.** To cook over boiling water in a covered pan, with the food suspended on a cooking rack above the water.

- **Stir.** To mix ingredients with a wooden spoon in a circular motion until well blended.
- **Toss.** To combine ingredients with a gentle lifting and dropping motion, using two implements.
- **Whisk.** To beat rapidly with a wire whisk to quickly and thoroughly blend liquid ingredients.

Simple Cooking Techniques

Even though this book focuses on the grill, some components of the preparation and presentation involve other kitchen skills.

Blanching

Some recipes call for blanching, which cooks vegetables or fruits for a minute or two before peeling them or adding them to a recipe. Depending on the vegetable, this will loosen the skin so it can be easily peeled, or it will brighten the colour of the vegetable to make it more attractive in the recipe.

To blanch, place a few litres of water on to boil in a large stockpot. Wash the vegetables or fruits and leave them whole or prepare as called for in the recipe. Drop the vegetable or fruit in the boiling water for several minutes – individual recipes will give you the exact time – then plunge them into ice-cold water to stop the cooking.

To peel tomatoes, for instance, blanch the tomatoes, then simply slip the loose skin from the flesh and use the peeled tomato as called for in the particular recipe. For vegetables such as green beans, blanch them, then drain them and set aside until needed.

Cooking Dried Beans

Cooked dried beans are a wonderful source of protein and a key ingredient in many recipes. tinned beans are readily available, but the texture and flavour of freshly cooked beans are far superior. Time permitting, follow the simple procedure described below to cook dried beans.

Sort through the beans first to find and discard any small pebbles, dirt clods, or other foreign objects. Discard any beans that look mouldy or shriveled. Rinse the beans in a colander to remove surface dirt, then transfer them to a large stockpot.

The smaller dried legumes, such as lentils and split peas, can be cooked without presoaking. Cover them with water and cook over medium heat for 30 minutes to an hour.

Larger beans, such as black beans or cannellini beans, need to be presoaked before cooking. To presoak, cover the beans with fresh water to a depth of about 12cm. Cover the pot and allow the beans to soak at room temperature for several hours or overnight. If you are pressed for time, cover the beans with several inches of water as described above, then bring the pot to a boil over high heat. Immediately turn off the heat and allow the beans to sit with the pot covered for about an hour.

When you are ready to cook the beans, drain off the soaking liquid and add enough fresh water to cover the beans by about 6cm. Bring to a boil over high heat, reduce the heat to medium, and simmer gently until the beans are tender but not mushy. The cooking time will vary depending on the type of bean, but plan on an hour or longer. Check the pot and add more water, as needed, to keep the beans fully submerged.

You may cook beans in large batches and keep them on hand in the refrigerator for several days or freeze them in premeasured amounts for future use.

Cooking Grains

Grains are easy to cook, and they're delicious when served as a part of a barbecued meal. Whole grains provide complex carbohydrates as well as vitamins, minerals, and fibre.

Different varieties of rice are called for in this book, each with slightly different cooking times that vary from 20 to 45 minutes, depending on the variety. Some rice, such as basmati, needs to be rinsed before cooking. Rice is added to rapidly boiling water, the typical ratio being 200g rice to 400ml water. The pan is then tightly covered as the rice simmers over very low heat until the grain has absorbed all of the water and is plump and tender. When the rice is done, turn off the heat and set the pot aside, with the lid in place, for at least 5 minutes or up to an hour before serving.

Bulgur is a quick-cooking cracked wheat. Add it to boiling water, stir, cover the pot, and cook over very low heat for about 15 minutes. Turn off the heat and, without disturbing the lid, allow the pot to stand for 5 minutes before serving.

Measuring Ingredients

Perhaps the most fundamental technique of all is the art of measuring. Once you have spent enough time in the kitchen, you will be able to 'eyeball' a tbsp of finely chopped coriander or know which size lemon will yield 2 tbsps of freshly squeezed juice. Until then, follow these guidelines. Also, keep in mind that the methods are different for measuring liquid or dry ingredients.

To measure liquid ingredients, choose clear glass measuring cups that bear red marks to delineate quantities and have a pouring spout. Place the measuring cup on a level surface, pour in the liquid, and then check the desired amount at eye level. It is useful to have several measuring cups of the same size so that you can measure and hold multiple ingredients at the same time in different measuring cups.

Dry ingredients should be measured in nested plastic or metal measuring spoons that allow you to fill the spoon to the brim. Dip the appropriately sized spoon into the ingredient and scoop the dry ingredient into the spoon until it is overflowing. Hold the spoon over a plate and use a straight edge – such as the handle of a wooden spoon – to level it off.

Measuring spoons come in sets that usually range from $1/8$ tsp to 1 tbsp. It is useful to have several sets of measuring spoons because many recipes will call for measures of liquid and dry ingredients.

A set of kitchen scales are indispensable. Sometimes you will purchase an exact quantity at the market, or in a prepacked container, but more often you will need to measure the amount as needed. With the measuring bowl in place, use the adjusting mechanism to set the scale at precisely '0' before you place the ingredients you are weighing on it. If you are using a digital scale, follow the manufacturer's directions.

Reconstituting Dried Fruits or Vegetables

Reconstituting dried fruits or vegetables is a technique that really comes in handy. Simply place dried fruits, tomatoes, or mushrooms in a bowl and cover with hot water. Allow them to plump for 15 to 30 minutes, until they are chewable but not mushy. Remove the fruits, tomatoes, or mushrooms from the liquid and use as directed in the recipe. The soaking liquid may be reserved to use later in a soup or sauce.

Steaming Vegetables

Steamed vegetables are easy to prepare. Place a steamer tray in a large saucepan and add about 4cm of water. Place the pan over medium-high heat and add the vegetables to the steamer tray. Cover the pan tightly and cook until fork-tender, meaning they are easily pierced with a fork but are still firm enough to hold their shape. Steaming time will vary depending on the type of vegetable.

Toasting Nuts and Seeds

Nuts and seeds add flavour and texture to different preparations, and toasting them brings out the essential oils and adds a pleasant crunch. Place the raw, unsalted nuts or seeds in a single layer in a dry cast-iron frying pan over a medium-high heat on the stovetop. Shake the pan as the nuts or seeds heat through. When the nuts have darkened in colour to a golden brown and emit a wonderful roasted aroma, they are done. Immediately transfer them to a plate or bowl so they do not continue to cook in the hot pan. Set aside.

Ready to grill? In the chapters to come, you'll find recipes for delicious sauces and marinades, salsas and chutneys, and everything from hors d'oeuvres to desserts.

CHAPTER 2

Seasoning Sauces
and Marinades

Key ingredients play a very important role in creating delicious recipes. Some of the sauces and marinades in this chapter are available in commercial preparations, but the true satisfaction – time permitting – comes from preparing them from scratch, tailoring the seasonings to your liking.

Many of the marinades are quick to prepare and can be kept in the refrigerator for several weeks until needed. Keep the Honey-Ginger Marinade (page 27), Spicy Plum Sauce Marinade (page 30), and Garlic-Soy Marinade (page 29) on hand to make almost instant tofu kebabs or to use as the base for a stir-fry dish. You can use Fresh BBQ Sauce (page 31) and Black Bean Sauce (page 32) in your own favourite recipes as well as in the ones in this book. Use the seasoning sauces and marinades as the focal point to put together that instant meal on a busy week night.

Some of the recipes can be prepared months ahead of time and either frozen or put up in Kilner jars until needed. If you grow basil during the summer and have a bumper crop, prepare batches of Basil Pesto (page 23) and freeze it in small jars to enjoy during the winter. Place a slice of fresh lemon over the sauce before securing the lid to prevent oxidation. The Tomato Coulis (page 24) is sure to become a favourite, especially if you grow pear tomatoes. I like to prepare the sauce in the late summer and put it in pint jars. The sauce may also be placed in jars and frozen for several months. Make sure that you leave about 2cm of head room for expansion during the freezing process.

Blueberries are becoming much more available, and the Fresh Blueberry Sauce (page 33) is excellent over many of the barbecued fruit recipes in this book. It's also delicious served over plain yogurt or vanilla ice cream. The Boysenberry Sauce (page 33) can be served over dessert or breakfast dishes, or it can be used as an ingredient to create a colourful savoury sauce to serve over an entrée, such as Pistachio-Encrusted Tofu with Basmati Rice (page 143).

Basil Pesto

INGREDIENTS

90g fresh basil

120ml extra-virgin olive oil

35g pine nuts, toasted

4 cloves garlic, chopped

50g finely grated Parmesan
cheese

Pinch salt

Lemon slice

This is a time-tested pesto recipe. Grow basil every summer and prepare this recipe when the plants need to be snipped back. I like to prepare multiple batches, place the pesto in small jars, and freeze them to use over the winter months. Place a slice of lemon on top of the pesto – leaving about 1cm of headroom for expansion – seal tightly, and freeze.

In a food processor or blender, puree the basil with half the olive oil and the pine nuts and garlic. With the machine running, add the remaining olive oil in a thin stream to form a smooth paste. If the paste is too thick, add additional olive oil, a tbsp at a time. Add the Parmesan cheese and salt and pulse to combine. Use immediately or transfer to a small jar. Place a lemon slice over the top, cover, and refrigerate or freeze until needed.

Yield: 260g

Mint Pesto

INGREDIENTS

90g loosely packed fresh mint
leaves

30g loosely packed fresh flat-leaf
parsley

120ml extra-virgin olive oil

2 cloves garlic, chopped

I tbsp (15ml) freshly squeezed
lemon juice

Pinch salt

Lemon slice

This refreshing pesto will become a favourite drizzled over barbecued potatoes, vegetables, or steamed rice. It is best if used within 2 days of preparation. Mint is easy to grow: Plant it in an area where you want it to spread (and it will!) or contain it in a large pot.

In a food processor or blender, puree the mint and parsley with half of the olive oil and the garlic. With the machine running, add the remaining olive oil and the lemon juice in a thin stream to form a smooth paste. Add the salt and pulse to combine. If the paste is too thick, add additional olive oil, a tbsp at a time. Use immediately or transfer to a small jar. Place a lemon slice over the top, cover, and refrigerate until needed.

Yield: 175g

Tomato Coulis

This tomato sauce is delicious over pasta or barbecued polenta. You will also find it called for throughout this book. If fresh tomatoes are not in season, you may substitute one 900g tinned tomatoes.

INGREDIENTS

3 pounds (1.5 kilograms) pear
   tomatoes

I tbsp (35ml)
   olive oil

2 cloves garlic, finely chopped

3 tsps finely chopped fresh
   oregano

$^1/_2$ tsp salt

Put several litres of water on to boil in a large pot on the hob. Place the tomatoes in a blanching basket and put the basket in the water, or simply drop the tomatoes into the boiling water. Within a minute or two, when the tomato skins begin to split and pull away from the flesh, remove the tomatoes with a slotted spoon to bowl of cold water. When the tomatoes are cool enough to handle, peel off the skins and cut out the stem ends. Cut the tomatoes in half cross-wise and gently squeeze to remove the juicy seed pockets. Coarsely chop the tomatoes and place them in a bowl.

Heat the olive oil in a heavy-bottomed frying pan on the hob. Stir and sauté the garlic for several seconds, then add the tomatoes. Cook over medium-high heat, stirring frequently, for about 5 minutes. Add the oregano and salt. Continue to cook for several minutes until almost all of the liquid has reduced, yielding a thick sauce. Set aside until needed or transfer to a jar and store in the refrigerator for several days.

Yield: 470ml

Vegetable Stock

INGREDIENTS

2 medium unpeeled red potatoes,
    coarsely chopped

2 medium yellow onions, diced

1 red or green bell pepper, seeded
    and diced

2 ribs celery, chopped

225g mushrooms, chopped

200g assorted vegetables,
    chopped

6 cloves garlic, chopped

2 bay leaves

2 tsps dried basil

1 tsp dried thyme

1 tsp salt

$^1/_2$ tsp ground pepper

Any combination of vegetables, including fresh or dried mushrooms, and a variety of herbs can be included in a stock. The key is to balance the flavour because you do not want a specific vegetable to dominate. Use the stems, stalks, and outer lettuce leaves that you would otherwise throw away as part of your assorted vegetable mix. It is always good to add a potato or two to give the stock some body. You may freeze this in measured amounts to use as needed. Measurements are given here, but don't feel compelled to measure exactly.

Put 3 litres water in a large stockpot on the hob over a medium-high heat. Add all the ingredients. Bring to a boil. Reduce the heat to low and simmer, uncovered, for about an hour. Turn off the heat and allow the mixture to cool for about 15 minutes before straining into a separate pot. Set aside to use immediately or transfer to a container and refrigerate for several days or freeze for several months.

Yield: about 2.5 litres

Soy and Balsamic
Fusion Marinade

This mix of Asian and Mediterranean ingredients is wonderful with mushrooms and with tempeh dishes.

INGREDIENTS

60ml dry sake

45ml soy sauce

1 tbsp (15ml) dark sesame oil

1 tbsp (15ml)
   balsamic vinegar

1 tbsp (15ml)
   vegetarian Worcestershire sauce

1 clove garlic, finely chopped

$^1/_4$ tsp dried tarragon

Place the sake, soy sauce, sesame oil, balsamic vinegar, and Worcestershire sauce in a medium bowl and whisk together. Add the garlic and tarragon and whisk to combine. Use the sauce immediately or refrigerate until needed.

Yield: 120ml

Honey-Ginger *Marinade*

Many different ingredients are delicious when marinated in this mixture. I especially like it with tofu.

INGREDIENTS

6 tbsps (90ml) freshly squeezed
   lemon juice

3 tbsps (45ml)
   dark sesame oil

3 tbsps (45ml)
   soy sauce

3 tbsps (60g) honey

3 tsps finely chopped fresh ginger

3 cloves garlic, finely chopped

Prepare the marinade in a medium bowl by whisking together the lemon juice, sesame oil, soy sauce, honey, ginger, and garlic. Use the marinade immediately or refrigerate until needed.

Yield: 235ml

Raspberry Vinegar Marinade

INGREDIENTS

2 tbsps (28ml) raspberry vinegar

I tbsp (35ml))
   dark sesame oil

I tbsp (35ml))
   soy sauce

3 tsps maple syrup

You will find many uses for this marinade, especially with winter root vegetables.

Put the raspberry vinegar, sesame oil, soy sauce, and maple syrup in a small bowl and whisk to combine. Use the marinade immediately or refrigerate until needed.

Yield: 90ml

Garlic-Soy Marinade

This combination of flavours works well with tofu or squashes.

INGREDIENTS

120ml freshly squeezed orange
   juice

3 tbsps (45ml) toasted sesame oil

2 tbsps (30ml) soy sauce

3 cloves garlic, finely chopped

1 tsp dried basil, crushed

Prepare the marinade in a medium bowl by whisking together the orange juice, sesame oil, soy sauce, garlic, and basil. Use immediately as a marinade or refrigerate until needed.

Yield: 175ml

Spicy Plum Sauce Marinade

INGREDIENTS

75g plum sauce

60ml freshly squeezed lemon juice

2 tbsps (30ml)
  soy sauce

1 tsp dried red chilli flakes,
  crushed

Spicy and sweet, this marinade is a flavourful way to season tofu for the grill. Plum sauce, the base ingredient of this marinade, is available in Asian markets.

Place the plum sauce, lemon juice, soy sauce, and chilli flakes in a small bowl and whisk to combine. Use immediately or cover and refrigerate for several days.

Yield: 120ml

Fresh BBQ Sauce

INGREDIENTS

700g cherry tomatoes

2 tbsps (30ml) canola oil

1 medium onion, chopped

2 tbsps (16g) grated fresh ginger

6 tsps fermented black beans,
   rinsed

4 cloves garlic, finely chopped

2 serrano chillies, seeded and
   finely chopped

60ml rice wine vinegar

60ml soy sauce

2 tbsps (40g) honey

Several grinds black pepper,
   to taste

This flavourful sauce has many uses. Try it not only with tofu, as called for in this book, but also with potatoes or on top of scrambled eggs. You may use black treacle instead of honey for a flavour variation.

Place several litres of water in a stockpot on the hob and bring to a boil over high heat. Place the tomatoes in a blanching basket and put the basket in the water, or simply drop the tomatoes into the boiling water. Within a minute or two, when the tomato skins begin to split and pull away from the flesh, remove the tomatoes with a slotted spoon to a bowl of cold water. When the tomatoes are cool enough to handle, peel off the skins and coarsely chop. Set aside.

Place the canola oil in a large frying pan on the hob over medium-high heat and add the onion, ginger, fermented black beans, garlic, and serrano chillies. Cook for 8 to 10 minutes, stirring frequently. Add the tomatoes, reduce the heat to medium-low, and continue to cook for about 15 minutes. Add the rice wine vinegar, soy sauce, honey, and black pepper and cook for an additional 5 minutes. Remove from the heat and place in a food processor. Blend until smooth. Keep refrigerated until needed. This sauce will hold over in the refrigerator for about 2 weeks.

Yield: 950ml

Black Bean Sauce

INGREDIENTS

85g fermented black beans,
  not rinsed

60ml mirin

2 tbsps (30ml)
  soy sauce

1 tbsp (35ml)
  canola oil

1 tbsp (9g)
  brown sugar

3 cloves garlic, finely chopped

2 tsps grated fresh ginger

Pinch dried red chilli flakes

Fermented black beans can be found in Asian markets, packed in jars. You will also find them in many health food stores and well-stocked supermarkets. Depending on how you are going to use this sauce, you may leave the beans whole, chop them, or puree them. You can find mirin (rice wine) where you find the fermented black beans.

Place the fermented black beans, mirin, soy sauce, canola oil, brown sugar, garlic, ginger, and chilli flakes in a blender along with 3 tbsps (45ml) water. Puree until smooth. Place in a small jar and refrigerate until needed. This sauce will stay fresh in the refrigerator for about 2 weeks.

Yield: 90ml

Fresh Blueberry Sauce

As a variation, you may use raspberries or blackberries for this sauce. You can add more honey if the sauce is too tart. Use this sauce as the base for a reduction sauce or pour it over barbecued fruit desserts.

INGREDIENTS

290g fresh
   blueberries

85g honey

l tbsp (35ml) freshly squeezed
   lemon juice

1/4 tsp salt

1/2 tsp vanilla

Wash the blueberries and place them in a bowl. Use a masher or slotted spoon to crush them. Stir in the honey, lemon juice, and salt. Place the mixture in a small saucepan on the hob and bring to a boil over high heat. Boil for about a minute, stirring to make sure the bottom doesn't scorch. Add the vanilla. Remove the saucepan from the heat and set aside to cool.

Place a sieve over a bowl and pour the sauce into it. Mash the berries with the back of a wooden spoon to press all of the sauce into the bowl. Discard the berry pulp. Transfer the sauce to a jar and refrigerate until needed, for up to 4 weeks.

Yield: 235ml

Boysenberry Sauce

My friends Paul and Lizz Blaise have a boysenberry patch in their garden that yields a bumper crop every year. Lizz prepares this sauce and uses it over pancakes, waffles, and French toast or to flavour yogurt and ice cream.

INGREDIENTS

770g fresh
   boysenberries

200g sugar

Place the boysenberries and sugar in a large pan on the hob over medium-high heat and bring to a boil. Reduce to a slow boil and cook, covered, for about 45 minutes. Remove the lid, reduce the heat to medium-low, and continue to cook for about 2 hours, stirring occasionally. (The berries will break up as the sauce thickens.) Remove the pan from the heat and allow to cool. Place a large sieve over a bowl and pour the sauce into it. Mash the berries with the back of a wooden spoon to press all of the sauce into the bowl. Discard the berry pulp. Transfer the sauce to a jar and refrigerate until needed, for up to 4 weeks. The sauce may also be frozen.

Yield: 970g

CHAPTER 3

Salsas, Chutneys, and Dipping Sauces

These simple combinations of vegetables, fruits, condiments, and spices yield the 'secret sauce' component for many fantastic meals. I have recommended specific salsas, chutneys, and dipping sauces to accompany many of the recipes throughout the book, but you should feel free to experiment with mixing and matching to discover your own favourite combinations.

Some of these recipes, such as the Salsa Fresca (page 45), Creamy Horseradish Sauce (page 53), Barbecued Red Bell Pepper Mayonnaise (page 47), and the Dilled Yogurt and Sour Cream Sauce (page 51) can be prepared ahead of time and kept in closed containers in the refrigerator for several days. Chutney will also hold over in the refrigerator for up to a week. Other fresh fruit combinations are best prepared right before serving. The Peach and Blueberry Salsa (page 36), Guacamole (page 48), and Mango and Papaya Salsa with Jalapeños (page 37) are best prepared when the ingredients are at the height of the season and best served at room temperature.

Choose large, shallow bowls to serve salsas or chutneys in or place several smaller shallow bowls around the table. Serve the dipping sauces in individual ramekins or very small bowls so the diners can repeatedly dip into their own serving of sauce.

Peach and Blueberry Salsa

INGREDIENTS

2 medium white peaches, peeled, seeded,
   and diced

50g blueberries, halved

2 spring onions, finely chopped

I tbsp (35ml) olive oil

I tsp balsamic vinegar

2 tsps lime juice

$^1/_2$ tsp crushed garlic

3 tsps finely chopped fresh sage

6 tsps finely chopped fresh basil

The delicate white peaches pair with the richly coloured berries to carry the flavours of this salsa. Serve it with fajitas or skewered entrées or simply enjoy it with corn chips.

Gently combine the peaches, blueberries, and spring onions in a medium bowl.

In a separate bowl, whisk together the olive oil, balsamic vinegar, lime juice, garlic, sage, and basil. Pour over the peach mixture and toss to combine. Allow the flavours to blend at room temperature for about 1 hour before serving. Use immediately or refrigerate overnight.

Yield: Ikg

Mango and Papaya
Salsa with Jalapeños

This salsa's bite is soothed by the sweetness of the fruit. Try it with Tempeh, Pineapple, and Jalapeño Skewers (page 165) or Brie and Mango Quesadillas (page 194).

INGREDIENTS

I firm, ripe mango, peeled, seeded,
   and diced

280g peeled, seeded, and diced papaya

I45g blueberries, halved

4 spring onions, finely chopped

I0g finely chopped fresh basil

2 tbsps (30ml) olive oil

I tsp balsamic vinegar

I tbsp (35ml) lime juice

2 cloves garlic, finely chopped

2 jalapeño chillies, seeded
   and finely chopped

Gently combine the mango, papaya, blueberries, spring onions, and basil in a medium bowl.

In a separate bowl, whisk together the olive oil, balsamic vinegar, lime juice, garlic, and jalapeño chillies. Pour over the mango mixture and toss to combine. Allow the flavours to blend at room temperature for about 1 hour before serving. Use the salsa immediately or refrigerate overnight.

Yield: Ikg

Smooth Tomatillo Salsa

INGREDIENTS

455g fresh tomatillos, in the husk

40g finely chopped white onion

5g finely fresh coriander

I tbsp (35ml) freshly squeezed
   lime juice

I jalapeño chile, seeded
   and finely chopped

2 cloves garlic, finely chopped

¼ tsp salt

This salsa is smooth when first prepared, but once refrigerated it turns into a jelly-like consistency. To return it to a smooth salsa, bring it to room temperature and add a tbsp or so of warm water. Stir to combine.

Place the tomatillos, still in their husks, in a plastic bag and fill the bag with water. Seal and allow the tomatillos to soak for about 15 minutes.

Preheat the barbecue to high with a smoker box in place. Remove the tomatillos from the bag and place them on the grill. barbecue for 15 to 18 minutes, turning frequently. (The husks will char slightly, but they should not totally blacken.) Remove the tomatillos from the barbecue and set aside to cool. When the tomatillos are cool enough to handle, remove and discard the husks and place the tomatillos in a food processor. Pulse to chop and add the onion, coriander, lime juice, jalapeño chilli, garlic, and salt. Puree until smooth. Transfer to a serving bowl.

Yield: 500g

Pear and Avocado Salsa

INGREDIENTS

1 Bartlett pear, peeled, seeded, and diced

1 medium Haas avocado, seeded, peeled, and diced*

1 large jalapeño chilli, seeded and finely chopped

3 tsps finely chopped fresh coriander

3 tsps finely chopped fresh flat-leaf parsley

1 spring onion, finely chopped

1 tbsp (35ml) olive oil

1 tbsp (35ml) lime juice

$1/8$ tsp granulated garlic

Pinch salt

This salsa can be prepared any time of the year to enjoy as an appetizer or to serve with a skewered entrée. Have all of your other ingredients prepared and set aside before you peel and dice the pear so it doesn't turn brown. Haas avocados are the ones with pebbled dark green or black skin.

Place the pear, avocado, and jalapeño chilli in a medium bowl and gently toss to combine. Add the coriander, parsley, and spring onion, tossing to combine.

In a separate bowl, whisk together the olive oil, lime juice, garlic, and salt. Pour over the pear mixture and gently toss to combine. Allow the flavours to blend at room temperature for about 1 hour before serving.

Yield: 500g

* Cut the avocado in half, remove the pit, then slice the shell and spoon out the avocado.

Pear-Cantaloupe Salsa

INGREDIENTS

2 Bartlett pears, peeled, seeded,
  and diced

310g diced cantaloupe

2 tbsps (30ml) lemon juice

45g diced red bell pepper

6 tsps finely chopped fresh
  coriander

2 spring onions, finely chopped

75ml rice vinegar

The colours in this salsa are a feast for the eyes. Prepare it in the late summer when all of the ingredients are fresh at the farmers' market. Have all of your other ingredients prepared and set aside before you peel and dice the pears so they don't turn brown.

Place the pears and cantaloupe in a medium bowl and toss with the lemon juice. Add the bell peppers, coriander, and spring onions. Toss to combine. Drizzle the rice vinegar over the pear mixture, then toss to combine. Allow the flavours to blend at room temperature for about 1 hour before serving. Use the salsa immediately or refrigerate overnight.

Yield: 1kg

Peach and Pineapple Salsa
with Fresh Tarragon

INGREDIENTS

2 peaches, peeled, seeded,
   and diced

80g diced pineapple

30g diced green bell pepper

I spring onion, finely chopped

I jalapeño chilli, seeded and finely
   chopped

2 tsps sherry vinegar

I tsp finely chopped fresh tarragon

The sweet peaches and the slightly acidic pineapple combine to make this salsa a spring treat. The jalapeño adds just the right heat to the sweetness – add more jalapeño if you want the salsa to be spicier. You may also want to add more tarragon, depending on the fresh variety that is available to you. Taste and see!

Place the peaches, pineapple, bell pepper, spring onion, and jalapeño chile in a bowl and gently toss to combine.

In a separate bowl, whisk together the sherry vinegar and tarragon. Pour over the peach mixture and gently toss to combine. Allow the flavours to blend at room temperature for about 1 hour before serving.

Yield: 500g

Jícama and Mango Salsa
with Jalapeños

INGREDIENTS

240g peeled and diced jícama

1 firm, ripe mango, peeled, seeded, and diced

2 firm, ripe kiwis, peeled and diced

55g diced red onion

2 jalapeño chillies, seeded and finely diced

5 tsps finely chopped fresh coriander

3 tbsps (45ml) freshly squeezed lime juice

A crunchy root vegetable, Jícama can be found in ethnic supermarkets; substitute Jerusalem artichokes or water chestnuts otherwise. This salsa is great with chips, quesadillas, and tofu tacos. It's best used the day it's prepared.

Place the jícama, mango, kiwis, red onion, and jalapeño chillies in a medium bowl and toss to combine. Add the coriander and lime juice, gently toss again, and set aside until needed.

Yield: 1.5kg

Salsa Fresca

INGREDIENTS

4 Anaheim or mild green chillies

1.25kg pear tomatoes

60ml freshly squeezed lime juice

80g finely chopped white onion

4g finely chopped fresh coriander

2 cloves garlic, finely chopped

1/8 tsp salt

Tomatoes, chillies, and fresh coriander are the foundation of a great salsa. This one is simple to prepare. The recipe may be doubled or tripled if you like to put foods in Kilner jars and process to preserve. The quantity this recipe yields will stay fresh for about 10 days in the refrigerator.

Preheat the barbecue to high. Place the chillies directly on the barbecue and barbecue for 8 to 10 minutes, turning frequently. (The skins will blacken.) Remove the chillies from the barbecue and place in a plastic bag. Seal the bag and set aside to cool. When the chillies are cool enough to handle, peel off the charred skin and place the chillies on a cutting board. Slice the chillies lengthwise, removing the stem ends and seeds. Chop the chillies and set aside.

Place several litres of water in a large stock pot on the hob and bring to a boil over high heat. Place the tomatoes in a blanching basket and put the basket in the water, or simply drop the tomatoes into the boiling water. Within a minute or two, when the tomato skins begin to split and pull away from the flesh, remove the tomatoes with a slotted spoon to a bowl of cold water. When the tomatoes are cool enough to handle, peel off the skins and cut out the stem ends. Cut the tomatoes in half crosswise. Gently squeeze the tomatoes over the sink to remove the juicy seed pockets, then dice the tomatoes and place them in a bowl. Drain off any juice. Add the chopped chillies, lime juice, onion, coriander, garlic, and salt. Serve immediately or refrigerate until needed.

Yield: 1125g

Peanut Sauce

INGREDIENTS

2 tbsps (30g) creamy
   peanut butter

2 tbsps (30ml)
   freshly squeezed lemon juice

1 tbsp (20g) honey

1 tbsp (17g) light-
   coloured miso

1 tbsp (35ml) mirin (rice wine)

1 tsp (35ml) soy sauce

Peanut sauce is a wonderful complement to a tofu or tempeh dish. You will also enjoy this sauce with jícama slices, celery sticks, and baby carrots. This sauce may be covered and refrigerated overnight, but bring it back to room temperature before serving.

Place the peanut butter, lemon juice, honey, miso, mirin, and soy sauce in a medium bowl, along with 120ml hot water, and whisk together until smooth. Set aside until needed.

Yield: 90ml

Garlic-Herb Mayonnaise

INGREDIENTS

175g mayonnaise

2 tbsps (30ml) freshly squeezed
   lemon juice

3 tsps finely chopped fresh thyme

3 tsps finely chopped fresh
   flat-leaf parsley

6 tsps chopped fresh chives

1/2 tsp crushed garlic

3 to 4 drops Tabasco-style
   hot sauce

Try this for a fast, flavourful mayonnaise. It makes a yummy dip for barbecued veggies as well as a tasty spread for wraps and sandwiches.

Place the mayonnaise, lemon juice, thyme, parsley, chives, garlic, and hot sauce in a medium bowl and whisk to combine. Transfer to a serving dish and use immediately or cover and refrigerate for up to 2 days.

Yield: 175g

Barbecued Red Bell Pepper Mayonnaise

INGREDIENTS

1 red bell pepper

1 large egg yolk

235ml extra-virgin olive oil

2 tbsps (30ml) freshly squeezed
   lemon juice

1 tsp crushed garlic

Pinch salt

Several grinds black pepper,
   to taste

Yield: 700 g

Homemade mayonnaise elevates this common condiment to new heights. Once mastered, you can prepare many variations to serve as sauces or spreads. They will keep in the refrigerator for about a week.

Preheat the barbecue to high. Place the bell pepper directly on the barbecue and barbecue for 10 to 15 minutes, turning frequently. barbecue until the skin is charred black. Transfer the pepper to a plastic or paper bag, close the bag, and set aside for about 15 minutes.

Meanwhile, place the egg yolk in a blender and pulse briefly. With the blender running, add the olive oil in a steady stream. (The egg and oil will emulsify into a thick sauce.) Add the lemon juice, garlic, salt, and black pepper and pulse to combine.

When the bell pepper is cool enough to handle, peel off the charred skin and discard the seeds, stem, and white membrane. Coarsely chop the pepper and add to the blender. Pulse to blend for a few seconds to create a smooth mayonnaise. Transfer to a jar and refrigerate for an hour or up to 1 week before serving.

Guacamole

Guacamole is one of the signature dishes of Mexico, but those of us north of the border love this spicy avocado dip, too. This version is best prepared right before serving. Haas avocados are the ones with pebbled dark green or black skin.

INGREDIENTS

2 medium-ripe Haas avocados, seeded, peeled, and diced

2 tbsps (30ml) freshly squeezed lime juice

55g finely chopped white onion

I clove garlic, finely chopped

I medium jalapeño chilli, seeded and finely chopped

$1/4$ tsp ground cumin

$1/4$ tsp salt

55g cherry tomatoes, diced (about 6 cherry tomatoes)

Place the avocados in a bowl. Add the lime juice, onion, garlic, jalapeño chilli, cumin and salt and mash with a fork until no large chunks remain. Stir in the tomatoes. Serve immediately or set aside at room temperature for up to 1 hour.

Yield: 450g

Mexican Crema

A slightly soured cream that is often served in Mexico as a table condiment with fajitas and taco dishes. This sauce is found commercially prepared in ethnic supermarkets, but it can be simply prepared at home.

INGREDIENTS

235ml heavy whipping cream

I tbsp (35ml) buttermilk

Pour the cream into a small saucepan on the hob. Heat the cream over a very low heat to bring it to a luke-warm temperature. Stir in the buttermilk and transfer the mixture to a glass jar. Loosely set the lid on the jar, but do not tighten. Set the jar aside in a warm place – 28°to 32°C – for 12 to 24 hours. (The crema will culture, becoming somewhat thick.) Stir with a wooden spoon, tighten the lid, and refrigerate for about 4 hours to chill before serving. (The crema will continue to thicken a bit as it chills.) Keep refrigerated and use within 2 weeks of preparation.

Yield: 230g

Spicy Tahini Sauce

This sauce is delicious served over a pasta dish or as a dip for barbecued vegetables or tofu.

INGREDIENTS

235ml Vegetable Stock (page 25)

3 tbsps (45g toasted
    sesame tahini

2 tbsps (30ml) soy sauce

I tbsp (35ml) rice vinegar

I tbsp (8g) grated fresh ginger

I tbsp (20g) honey

$^1/_4$ tsp red chilli flakes, crushed

In a saucepan, whisk together the Vegetable Stock, tahini, soy sauce, rice vinegar, ginger, honey, and chilli flakes. Place on the hob and bring to a boil. Reduce the heat to medium-low and simmer for about 5 minutes. Set aside until needed.

Yield: 300g

Dilled Yogurt and Sour Cream Sauce

INGREDIENTS

125g low-fat plain yogurt

115g low-fat sour cream

1 tbsp (35ml) red wine vinegar

1 tsp (15g) dried dill weed, crushed

$1/2$ tsp crushed garlic

$1/8$ tsp salt

Several grinds black pepper, to taste

This sauce is very easy to prepare, and it is best made ahead of time so the flavours can blend. It is good with barbecued potatoes, vegetables, and tofu entrées.

Place the yogurt and sour cream in a small bowl and whisk in the red wine vinegar, dill, garlic, salt, and black pepper. When well combined, cover and refrigerate until needed. Uncover and serve or transfer to individual dipping bowls.

Yield: 235ml

Creamy Ponzu Sauce

INGREDIENTS

60ml ponzu sauce

30g sour cream

1 tbsp (35ml) freshly squeezed lime juice

Ponzu sauce is a citrus-seasoned soy sauce that you will find in Aisian supermarkets. Once you've bought the basic ponzu sauce, this is a very fast and easy sauce to prepare. Keep the ingredients on hand to whip this up to complement many barbecued dishes.

In a small bowl, whisk together the ponzu sauce, sour cream, and lime juice. Serve immediately or refrigerate until needed.

Yield: 90ml

Remoulade Sauce

This classic French sauce is easy to prepare and delicious with barbecued vegetables or spread on sandwiches.

INGREDIENTS

235g mayonnaise

1 tbsp (15g) Dijon mustard

2 tbsps (30g) sweet pickle relish

2 tbsps (15g) finely chopped capers

3 tsps finely chopped fresh tarragon

Place the mayonnaise in a small bowl and add the mustard, relish, capers, and tarragon. Stir until well combined. Place in a small jar and refrigerate until needed.

Yield: 300g

Creamy Horseradish Sauce

This sauce is wonderful with barbecued potatoes, eggplant, tofu, or tempeh.

INGREDIENTS

230g sour cream

1 tbsp (15g) ketchup

1 tbsp (35ml) freshly squeezed lemon juice

1 tsp vegetarian Worcestershire sauce

2 tsps prepared horseradish

Pinch salt

Several grinds black pepper, to taste

Place the sour cream in a bowl and whisk in the ketchup, lemon juice, Worcestershire sauce, horseradish, salt, and black pepper. Set aside in the refrigerator for 1 hour or up to overnight so the flavours can blend.

Yield: 300ml

CHAPTER 4

Hors d'Oeuvres, Dips, and Spreads

Hors d'oeuvres — French for appetizers, the food served at the beginning of the meal — go way beyond cheese and crackers or salsa and chips. Adding the grill as a cooking method opens the door to interesting appetizers, innovative dips, and savoury spreads. They can be casual or fancy in their presentation, eaten with fingers or a fork, and enjoyed standing up or sitting down. Serve a single hors d'oeuvre to begin a meal or serve several together for a fun cocktail party.

Most of these grilled hors d'oeuvres are simple to prepare. The recipes can be doubled to feed a crowd, and they can be made ahead of time, before your guests arrive, so you can spend more time enjoying the festivities. Mushrooms Stuffed with Couscous, Mint Pesto, and Walnuts (page 62), Crostini with Grilled Courgette and Eggplant (page 64), and Grilled Spinach Rolls Stuffed with Tofu and Feta (page 56) make a tasty finger-food buffet.

Get creative with the presentation by using pretty plates and bowls, edible flowers and herbs, and a colorful array of napkins. Set the hors d'oeuvres out where you want your guests to gather and serve your favourite libations. Prepare and stage the Purple Figs Stuffed with Blue Cheese (page 57) in advance, and then barbecue with your guests present for a bevy of comments about your barbecuing prowess. Barbecued Kalamata Olives (page 61) are especially fun to prepare with your guests surrounding the barbecue area.

Many of the dips and spreads in this chapter will keep fresh for several days in the refrigerator, ready to be brought out on a weeknight and nibbled on when you arrive home from work. The Hummus with Grilled

Garlic (page 78) and the Cannellini Bean Spread with Grilled
Red Peppers (page 79) will both keep for several days in the
refrigerator, so they are great choices to enjoy as a pre-prepared,
instant snack. We must remember to pamper ourselves with
good food and make it easily accessible to family and friends,
rather than just saving it for special occasions.

Lettuce Wraps
with Barbecued Peppers and Kalamata Olives

This appetizer has a Greek theme and is easy to prepare. It is low in carbohydrates but big in flavour.

INGREDIENTS

1 large red bell pepper

12 large lettuce leaves
  (not iceberg)

115g crème fraîche

115g soft goat cheese

25g chopped kalamata olives

6 teaspoons snipped fresh
  oregano

Several grinds black pepper,
  to taste

Yield: 6 side-dish servings

Preheat the barbecue to high. Place the bell pepper directly on the barbecue and grill for 10 to 15 minutes, turning frequently. (The skin will be charred black.) Transfer the pepper to a plastic or paper bag, close the bag, and set aside for about 15 minutes.

Meanwhile, wash the lettuce leaves, carefully spin them dry in a salad spinner or shake off the water, and place them on a towel to dry. Set aside.

When the bell pepper is cool enough to handle, peel off the charred skin and discard the seeds, stem, and white membrane. Chop the pepper and place it in medium bowl along with the crème fraîche and goat cheese. Mix with a wooden spoon to combine. Add the olives, oregano, and black pepper and then mix to combine.

Place a lettuce leaf, cupped side up, on a work surface. Spoon one-twelfth of the pepper mixture slightly off-centre on the leaf. Wrap in the sides of the leaf and place seam side down on a serving plate. Repeat the process with the remaining leaves and pepper mixture. If not serving immediately, you can hold them over in the refrigerator for an hour or so.

Purple Figs
Stuffed with Blue Cheese

INGREDIENTS

8 large, firm, ripe purple figs

45g crumbled blue cheese

4 thin slices rustic country loaf
   bread, cut into triangles

This simple appetizer is a seasonal treat, so prepare and serve it often at the height of fig season in late summer. Choose figs that are firmly ripe so that they hold up on the barbecue. There may be a small amount of the filling left over after you fill the figs. Spread it on bread and enjoy while you barbecue the figs.

Preheat the barbecue to medium-high. Cut the stem end from each fig about one-third of the way down and set aside. Hollow out the seed pulp and place in a small bowl. Add the blue cheese to the pulp and mix to combine. Carefully stuff the cheese mixture back into the hollowed-out figs and put the reserved stem end on top of each fig.

   Place the figs upright on the grill rack and place the rack on the barbecue. Barbecue for about 5 minutes, until the cheese begins to melt and the caps start to rise.

   Meanwhile, place the bread on the barbecue to toast for 2 to 4 minutes, turning as necessary. Continue to barbecue the figs for about 2 minutes, then carefully remove using a spatula and tongs. (Do not squeeze the figs too much, or you will force the filling out.) Place 2 figs on each serving plate and arrange barbecueed bread alongside. Serve immediately.

Yield: 4 side-dish servings

Barbecued Spinach Rolls
Stuffed with Tofu and Feta

INGREDIENTS

12 large leaves spinach or chard

140g firm-style silken tofu

115g crumbled feta cheese

$1/4$ tsp granulated garlic

$1/8$ tsp freshly grated nutmeg

Several grinds black pepper,
   to taste

12 long, thick fresh chives

$1/2$ tsp olive oil

2 lemons, cut in wedges

Choose large spinach leaves or use early spring Swiss chard for this recipe. The preparation is simple and may be done in advance. Prepare the rolls as an appetizer for a barbecue party or serve them as a side dish.

Preheat the barbecue to medium-high. Wash the spinach or chard and remove the thick stems, taking care not to tear the leaves. Pat them dry with paper towels.

Rinse the tofu and pat dry with paper towels. Cut the tofu into cubes and place in a food processor along with the feta cheese, garlic, nutmeg, and black pepper. Pulse to combine. (The resulting mixture should still be a bit lumpy.) Place a spinach leaf on a work surface and spoon one-twelfth of the filling into the centre, tuck in the sides, and roll up. Tie one of the chives around the bundle to secure it. Repeat this process to make the rest of the rolls.

Coat your hands with the olive oil and gently rub each roll. Place them on a cold barbecue tray, then place the tray on the barbecue. Barbecue for about 8 to 10 minutes, turning, to heat through. Serve immediately, passing the lemon.

Yield: 6 side-dish servings

Aubergine with Ricotta
and Tomato Coulis

Serve a good crusty bread to mop up the sauce.

INGREDIENTS

2 medium aubergines

120ml olive oil

500g ricotta cheese

6 teaspoons finely chopped
   fresh oregano

$1/4$ teaspoon salt

Several grinds black pepper,
   to taste

470ml Tomato Coulis (page 24)

Preheat the barbecue to medium-high. Remove the stem ends of the aubergines. Cut them lengthwise into 2cm slices. Use a pastry brush to coat one side with some of the olive oil and place oil sides down on the barbecue. Grill for 4 to 6 minutes, brush the top sides with the remaining oil, turn, and grill for 3 to 5 minutes. (The aubergine should be slightly soft with grill marks but not completely blackened.) Remove the aubergine to a cutting board.

Meanwhile, combine the ricotta cheese with the oregano, salt, and black pepper in a bowl.

Place the Tomato Coulis in a small saucepan over a medium-low heat.

Working with one slice of aubergine at a time, place some of the ricotta mixture in the centre and roll over the ends. Repeat with the remaining slices. Place the aubergine rolls, seam side down, on a platter or individual serving plates. Pour the warm Tomato Coulis over the top and serve immediately.

Yield: 8 side-dish servings

Basil-Pesto Stuffed Mushrooms

INGREDIENTS

12 large button mushrooms

1 tbsp (14ml) olive oil

55g breadcrumbs

65g Basil Pesto (page 23)

60g low-fat plain yogurt

2 tbsps (30g) low-fat sour cream

3 tsps pine nuts, chopped

Serve this easy, elegant appetizer hot off the barbecue, placed on a platter, drizzled with a bit of olive oil and garnished with some fresh basil leaves. Or you can pack the mushrooms in a container in a single layer and enjoy them on your next picnic.

Brush any dirt from the mushrooms and carefully snap off the stem ends. Reserve the stems for another use. Lightly oil the mushroom tops with the olive oil and set them aside on a plate.

Preheat the barbecue to medium-high. Place the breadcrumbs, Basil Pesto, yogurt, and sour cream in a bowl and mix to combine. Spoon equal amounts into the cavity of each mushroom and top with the pine nuts. Place the mushrooms on a barbecue rack and transfer to the barbecue. Barbecue for 10 minutes until the mushrooms are moist and tender. Transfer the mushrooms to a platter or individual small plates. Serve immediately.

Yield: 12 side-dish servings

Barbecued Kalamata Olives

INGREDIENTS

200g kalamata olives

1 tbsp (14ml) olive oil

3 tsps finely chopped fresh thyme

This simple dish is a common appetizer served in countries throughout the Mediterranean. Any salt-cured black olive may be used, although the kalamata variety is commonly available. If you are going to use the olives as an ingredient in a recipe, pit them first, then proceed with barbecuing.

Place the olives in a bowl and drizzle with the olive oil. Sprinkle with the thyme and toss to combine. Marinate for about 45 minutes, tossing occasionally.

Preheat the barbecue to medium-high with a smoker box in place. Put the olives in a barbecueing basket and grill for 4 to 5 minutes, stirring frequently. (The olives will darken slightly and wrinkle.)

Remove the olives from the barbecue and place in a serving bowl with a smaller bowl for the pits alongside. Let the olives cool for several minutes before serving because the pits will be very hot.

Yield: 16 side-dish servings

Mushrooms Stuffed with
Couscous, Mint Pesto, and Walnuts

INGREDIENTS

60g chopped raw, unsalted
   walnuts

60g uncooked couscous

12 large button mushrooms

1 tbsp (14ml) olive oil

150g Mint Pesto (page 23)

80g low-fat plain yogurt

2 tbsps (30g) low-fat sour cream

A stuffed mushroom is the perfect composed appetizer. This one is best served on a small plate with a fork.

Place the walnuts in a single layer in a dry heavy-bottomed frying pan over medium-high heat. Shake the pan frequently until the nuts are golden brown and emit a wonderful roasted aroma. Immediately remove the walnuts from the pan and set aside.

Place 150ml water in a small saucepan on the hob over high heat and bring to a boil. Add the couscous, stir, cover, and remove from the heat. Set aside for 5 minutes.

Preheat the barbecue to medium-high. Brush any dirt from the mushrooms and carefully snap off the stem ends. Reserve the stems for another use. Lightly oil the mushroom tops with the olive oil and set them aside on a platter, gill side up.

Stir the Mint Pesto, yogurt, and sour cream into the couscous. Fill each mushroom cavity with equal amounts of the couscous mixture and top with the toasted walnuts.

Place the mushrooms on a grill rack and transfer to the barbecue. Grill for 10 minutes, until the mushrooms are moist and tender. Transfer the mushrooms to a platter or individual small plates. Serve immediately.

Yield: 12 side-dish servings

Barbecued Artichokes
with Lemon Butter and Summer Savoury

2 medium artichokes

I tsp (14ml) olive oil

2 tbsps (28g) unsalted butter

I tsp finely chopped fresh
    summer savoury or thyme

Pinch salt

I tbsp (14ml freshly squeezed
    lemon juice

8 slices Italian-style country bread

Placing these artichokes on the barbecue to finish the cooking gives them a delightful smoky flavour. You may brush the artichokes with olive oil or use a spray oil to coat them. Pass fresh crusty bread to sop up the sauce.

Snap off the small, tough outer leaves at the base of the artichokes. Trim off about 1cm of the sharp points from the mid-range leaves and from the top. Trim about 2cm from the base of the stem. Put a steamer rack in a large saucepan that has a tight-fitting lid and place the artichokes on the rack, leaves pointing down. Add several centimetres of water to the saucepan and cover tightly. Place the saucepan on the hob and bring the water to a boil, reduce the heat to medium, and steam for about 25 minutes until the bottoms of the artichokes are tender but not soft. Remove the artichokes from the saucepan to a cutting board. Let the artichokes cool for several minutes. Cut each artichoke in half lengthwise with a sharp knife. Spoon out and discard the choke (the fuzzy fibres), leaving the leaves attached to the bottom.

    Preheat the barbecue to medium-high. Rub the cut sides of the artichokes with the olive oil and place cut sides down on the barbecue. Grill for 1 to 2 minutes on each side to heat through and create grill marks.

    Meanwhile, melt the butter in a small pan on the hob and add the herbs and salt. Remove the pan from the heat and stir in the lemon juice. Arrange the artichokes on a serving platter or individual appetizer plates. Drizzle with the butter mixture and set aside for a few minutes so some of the butter will soak in. Serve while still warm, with the bread.

Yield: 4 side-dish servings

Crostini
with Fresh Tomatoes, Basil, and Garlic

INGREDIENTS

3 medium tomatoes

45g fresh basil

2 tbsps (15g) chopped capers

2 tbsps (28ml) extra-virgin
  olive oil

2 tsps freshly squeezed
  lemon juice

3 cloves garlic, finely chopped

Pinch salt

I French baguette

Crostini – toasted bread slices – are wonderful to prepare during the summertime on the barbecue. All of the topping ingredients you'll need are in season, and your guests can join in the preparation. I like to use a baguette, but you may use another shape of bread and cut the slices into smaller pieces.

Cut the tomatoes in half crosswise and squeeze out the seed pockets. Cut out and discard the stem ends. Dice the tomatoes and place in a bowl.

Chop the basil or roll up the leaves and cut chiffonade-style (see page 16 for this technique) into paper-thin shreds. Add the basil to the bowl along with the capers and toss to combine.

In another bowl, whisk together the olive oil, lemon juice, garlic, and salt. Drizzle over the tomato mixture and toss to combine. Set aside at room temperature until ready to serve.

Meanwhile, preheat the barbecue to medium. Cut the baguette into $1/2$-inch slices. Arrange the bread on the grill rack in a single layer. Barbecue for 1 to 2 minutes per side until the bread is lightly browned and crisp on the outside, but still soft and chewy on the inside, creating perfect crostini. Set aside.

To serve, place a spoonful of the tomato mixture on top of each slice of crostini and serve on a platter or allow your guests to serve themselves, mounding the tomato mixture onto single slices of crostini.

Yield: 12 side-dish servings

Crostini
with Barbecued Courgette and Aubergine

INGREDIENTS

4 medium courgettes

2 aubergines

2 tbsps (28ml) olive oil

4 cherry tomatoes

3 tbsps (45mll) extra-virgin
   olive oil

2 tbsps (28ml) balsamic vinegar

3 tsps finely chopped
   fresh oregano

3 tsps finely chopped fresh basil

I tsp finely chopped fresh thyme

$^1/_8$ tsp salt

Several grinds black pepper,
   to taste

2 French baguettes

During the summer months, every gardener who has planted courgettes and aubergine is constantly looking for new ways to prepare the yields from these bountiful crops. You may cut this recipe in half if you are not entertaining guests or simply keep the left-overs to enjoy the next day.

Preheat the barbecue to medium-high. Remove the ends from the courgette and discard. Slice the courgettes lengthwise. Remove the stem ends from the aubergines and discard. Slice the aubergines lengthwise. Place the courgettes and aubergines in a plastic bag and drizzle with the olive oil. Twist the bag to seal, allowing some air to remain in the bag. Toss gently to coat the vegetables evenly. Place the courgette and aubergines on the barbecue and grill for 8 to 10 minutes, turning frequently. Remove all of the courgette and aubergine from the barbecue and set aside on a cutting board to cool for several minutes. When the courgette and aubergine are cool enough to handle, chop and set aside.

Meanwhile, remove the cores from the tomatoes and discard. Cut the tomatoes in half and gently squeeze to remove the seed pockets. Chop the tomatoes and set aside in a large bowl. Add the chopped courgette and aubergine.

In a small bowl, whisk together the extra-virgin olive oil, balsamic vinegar, oregano, basil, thyme, salt, and black pepper. Drizzle over the tomato and barbecueed vegetable mixture and toss to combine.

Cut the baguette into $^1/_2$-inch slices. Arrange the slices on the grill rack in a single layer. Barbecue for about 2 minutes per side until the bread is lightly browned and crisp on the outside, but still soft and chewy on the inside, creating perfect crostini. Set aside.

To serve, place a spoonful of the vegetable mixture on top of each slice of crostini and serve on a platter or allow your guests to serve themselves, mounding the vegetable mixture onto single slices of crostini.

Yield: 24 side-dish servings

Bruschetta

Bruschetta is Italian-style garlic bread. Be sure to choose a good, fruity olive oil for the most flavourful results.

INGREDIENTS

6 tbsps (90ml extra-virgin olive oil

4 cloves garlic, finely chopped

I loaf thick-crusted bread

Preheat the barbecue to medium. Whisk together the olive oil and garlic in a small bowl. Set aside.

If using a baguette-shaped loaf, cut it into $1/2$-inch slices. If using a dome-shaped loaf, cut it in half, then cut each half into $1/2$-inch slices. Place the bread on the barbecue. Cook for about 2 minutes per side until the bread is lightly browned and crisp on the outside, but still soft and chewy on the inside. Remove the bread from the barbecue and brush one side with the oil and garlic mixture. Serve immediately.

Yield: I2 side-dish servings

Garlic Jam

Cooking whole garlic bulbs transforms the cloves into a pungent paste that can be spread on bread or used as an ingredient in many recipes. Keep some on hand to use as an ingredient. The smoky, mellow flavour is quite distinct from that of raw garlic.

INGREDIENTS

2 large bulbs fresh garlic

$1/4$ tsp olive oil

8 sprigs fresh flat-leaf parsley

1 loaf thick-crusted bread, sliced

Preheat the barbecue to medium. Rub the papery skin from the garlic, but do not break them into individual cloves. Cut about 1cm off the pointed top ends of the bulbs and rub the cut surfaces with the olive oil. Place the garlic bulbs, cut sides up, in a covered clay or glass baking dish and place on the barbecue. (You could wrap the garlic in foil. Then place the foil packet on a baking stone or on baking bricks so the garlic cooks but does not burn on the bottom.) Grill for about 45 minutes. When the garlic feels very soft when gently squeezed, remove from the barbecue. Place the garlic on a serving dish and let cool for several minutes.

Gently pull the garlic cloves apart, leaving them attached to the base of the bulbs. Place the garlic on a serving platter and garnish with the parsley. Place the bread in a basket. To remove the garlic from the skin, squeeze a clove from the bottom, allowing the garlic jam to slide out from the cut end onto the slices of bread. Serve with a lot of napkins because this is finger food.

Yield: 12 side-dish servings

Barbecued Pita Triangles

INGREDIENTS

6 rounds whole wheat pita bread

4 tbsps (60ml)

   olive oil

These pita bread 'chips' are great by themselves, but also wonderful with a variety of dips or spreads. Watch carefully while the chips are barbecuing because they will burn to a crisp if unattended.

Preheat the barbecue to medium. Cut each pita-bread round into quarters, then separate the layers to create 8 triangles per round. Lightly brush or spray the pita bread with the olive oil and place directly on the barbecue. Grill for about 5 minutes, turning frequently until both sides are slightly toasted. Place in a basket and serve.

Yield: 24 side-dish servings

Hummus
with Barbecued Garlic

Hummus – chickpea spread – has many variations, but his is my favourite. Serve with Barbecued Pita Triangles (page 69), sesame crackers, or fresh vegetables. This spread will keep refrigerated for several days.

INGREDIENTS

1 bulb garlic

¼ tsp olive oil

325g cooked chickpeas

75ml freshly squeezed
  lemon juice

60g toasted sesame tahini

2 tbsps (28ml) extra-virgin
  olive oil

2 spring onions, finely chopped

½ tsp salt

Preheat the barbecue to medium. Rub the papery skin from the garlic, but do not break it into individual cloves. Cut about 1cm off the pointed top end of the bulb and rub the cut surface with the olive oil. Place the garlic bulb, cut side up, in a covered clay or glass baking dish and place on the barbecue, and grill for about 45 minutes. (You could wrap the garlic in foil. Then place the foil packet on a baking stone or on baking bricks so the garlic cooks but does not burn on the bottom.) When the garlic feels very soft when gently squeezed, remove from the barbecue. When cool enough to handle, squeeze the garlic paste from the individual cloves into a small bowl and set aside.

Place the chickpeas, lemon juice, tahini, extra-virgin olive oil, and 1 tbsp (14ml) water in a blender or food processor and puree until smooth. (Add a tbsp or two more of water if the mixture is too thick.) Add the spring onions, barbecueed garlic, and salt, and pulse to combine.

Transfer the hummus to a serving dish and serve immediately or refrigerate for up to several days. Serve at room temperature.

Yield: 18 side-dish servings

Cannellini Bean Spread
with Barbecued Red Pepper

INGREDIENTS

I large red bell pepper

700g tin cannellini beans

I tbsp (14ml)
   extra-virgin olive oil

I tbsp (14ml)
   fresh-squeezed lemon juice

6 tsps finely chopped fresh basil

$^1/_2$ tsp salt

You can find dried cannellini beans in any natural food store or Italian market and can easily soak and cook them. For convenience, they are also available precooked, sold in 700g tins in many markets, and that's what I used in this recipe. Serve this spread on crackers or bread. It is also delicious as a sandwich spread.

Preheat the barbecue to high. Place the bell pepper directly on the barbecue and grill for 10 to 15 minutes, turning frequently. (The skin will be charred black.) Transfer the pepper to a plastic or paper bag, close the bag, and set aside for about 15 minutes. When the pepper is cool enough to handle, peel off the charred skin and discard the stem, seeds, and white membrane. Coarsely chop.

   Place the barbecued pepper, cannellini beans, 2 tbsps (28ml) water, olive oil, lemon juice, basil, and salt in a food processor. Pulse to combine. Transfer to a serving bowl and serve immediately or refrigerate overnight.

Yield: 10 appetizer servings

BBQ Aubergine Spread

INGREDIENTS

2 medium aubergines

4 spring onions, finely chopped

2 cloves garlic, finely chopped

15g finely chopped fresh parsley

6 tsps finely chopped fresh
  oregano

$^1/_4$ tsp salt

Several grinds black pepper,
  to taste

60ml extra-virgin olive oil

3 tbsps (45ml) freshly squeezed
  lemon juice

I first enjoyed a version of this dish, also called baba ghanouj, on the Greek island of Mykonos. This recipe may not be authentic, but it is delicious and duplicates the flavours I savoured that day. Serve this spread as an appetizer with crusty bread or as a side salad.

Preheat the barbecue to medium-high. Place the aubergines on the barbecue and grill for about 1 hour. Turn the aubergines several times as they cook. (The skins will become charred and the aubergines will become very soft.) Remove the aubergines from the barbecue and set aside to cool. When the aubergines are cool enough to handle, cut off the stem ends and peel away the skin. Drain off any liquid. Coarsely chop the aubergine and transfer it to a food processor. Add the spring onions, garlic, parsley, oregano, salt, and black pepper. Pulse to combine, achieving a chunky – not perfectly smooth – texture. Add the olive oil and lemon juice and pulse to combine. Transfer to a serving bowl and serve immediately or allow the flavours to blend at room temperature for an hour or so.

Yield: 12 appetizer servings

Jicama and Barbecued Red Peppers

INGREDIENTS

1 large red bell pepper

1 small jícama

2 tbsps (28ml) freshly squeezed
   lime juice

1 tsp mild chilli powder

$1/8$ tsp salt

This refreshing appetizer is delightfully simple. It can be prepared ahead of time and refrigerated until serving. One of the wonderful qualities of jícama is that it retains its crispness for several days – even after it is cut. Substitute water chestnuts if you can't find jícama.

Preheat the barbecue to high. Place the bell pepper directly on the barbecue and grill for 10 to 15 minutes, turning frequently. (The skin will be charred black.) Transfer the pepper to a plastic or paper bag, close the bag, and set aside for about 15 minutes. When the pepper is cool enough to handle, peel off the charred skin and discard the seeds, stem, and white membrane. Dice the pepper and set aside.

Meanwhile, peel the jícama and cut it in half from stem to root. Place each piece cut side down on a cutting board and cut into $1/2$-cm slices. Place the slices in a bowl and drizzle with the lime juice. Toss to combine.

On a pretty plate, make a ring of overlapping slices of jícama, retaining the lime juice in the bowl. Mound the diced pepper in the centre of the ring. Drizzle the reserved lime juice evenly over the jícama and bell pepper, then dust the jícama with the chilli powder and salt.

Serve immediately or cover with clingfilm and refrigerate overnight. Place a small fork on the plate before serving. To serve, allow diners to place a small mound of bell pepper on a jícama slice and eat with their fingers.

Yield: 8 appetizer servings

CHAPTER 5

Salads and Side Dishes

Barbecuing adds a delicious flavour to vegetable side dishes and, surprisingly, many salads as well. And it's so convenient to create the entire meal out at the barbecue rather than running back and forth to the stove. You'll be delighted with the range of salad and side-dish recipes in this chapter.

Spring gardens and local farmers' markets bring us an abundance of fresh lettuce leaves, thus providing the perfect mix of greens. During the summer and winter months – depending on your climate – you can grow a fresh salad mix or rely on the world market to provide for your culinary needs through your local supermarket.

Some of the recipes in this chapter call for tossed leaf greens with barbecued vegetables or fruits. Many should be enjoyed at the peak of the season for the particular ingredient, like the Spinach Salad with Barbecued Peaches and Gorgonzola Cheese (page 80), Red Lettuce Salad with Barbecued Beets and Goats Cheese (page 79), or the Iceberg Lettuce with Barbecued Figs and Creamy Blue Cheese Dressing (page 82). Ingredients for other salads, such as Caesar Salad with Smoky Barbecued Tofu (page 81) or Fresh Greens with Barbecued Hearts of Palm (page 76), can be prepared year-round. The dressings rely on a good olive oil and fresh lemon juice or wine vinegars, alongside finely chopped fresh herbs.

Not all of the salads in this chapter call for greens. Some rely on more hearty ingredients, like beans or pasta, as the base. Enjoy the Corn, Black Bean, and Avocado Salad (page 84) or the Pasta Salad with Barbecued Radicchio and Sweet Peppers (page 85) all year. Many of these salads can be a light meal all by themselves when served with bread, crackers, or chips.

I think of side-dish vegetables as seasonal for the most part. Spring has arrived when the first locally grown asparagus shows up at the farmers' market. You'll want to prepare the Asparagus with Watercress Sauce (page 88) often and consider serving it as part of a spring or Easter buffet. Summer has an abundance of vegetables, most of which are delicious barbecued. Barbecuing corn in its husk allows the kernels to steam and become tender-crisp – and no flavour is lost to the boiling pot of water! White Corn with Chilli Butter (page 94) is sure to become a seasonal favourite. Barbecued courgette is an old standby, so be sure to try the Summer Squashes with Lemon Basil (page 92). When you include the Aussie Chips with Sweet Chilli Sauce (page 98) and Barbecued Red Potatoes (page 96) in your repertoire, you have seasonless side-dish selections coming hot from your barbecue.

BBQ Endive salad
with Golden Raisins

Endive is a slightly bitter lettuce, firm enough to stand up to the barbecue's heat. The leaves slightly wilt and take on the fire's flavours.

INGREDIENTS

35g pine nuts

3 tbsps (45ml) extra-virgin olive oil

1 tbsp (14ml) balsamic vinegar

$^1/_2$ tsp honey

$^1/_2$ tsp Dijon mustard

Pinch salt

Several grinds black pepper, to taste

2 Belgian endives, halved lengthwise

1 tbsp (14ml) olive oil

170g loosely packed torn red lettuce
    leaves

35g golden raisins

Place a single layer of pine nuts in a small cast-iron frying pan on the hob over medium-high heat. Shake the pan frequently. (The nuts will become slightly golden and emit a nutty aroma.) Remove the nuts from the pan and set aside until needed.

In a small bowl, whisk together the extra-virgin olive oil, balsamic vinegar, honey, mustard, salt, and black pepper. Set the dressing aside.

Meanwhile, preheat the barbecue to medium-high. Use a pastry brush to brush both sides of the endive with some of the olive oil. Place the endive on the barbecue, cut sides down. Cook for about 2 minutes, baste with some more of the oil, and turn with tongs. Continue to cook for about 2 more minutes. (The endive will wilt slightly and develop barbecue marks.) Remove the endive from the barbecue.

Place the lettuce in a large bowl and drizzle with the dressing. Toss to combine. Distribute between 4 salad plates. Place one barbecued endive half atop the lettuce on each plate. Sprinkle with equal amounts of raisins and pine nuts. Serve immediately.

Yield: 4 side-dish servings

Mixed Greens
with Barbecued Summer Vegetables and Blue Cheese

INGREDIENTS

1 medium yellow butternut squash

1 medium courgette

1 Japanese aubergine

1 tbsp (14ml) olive oil

60ml extra-virgin olive oil

2 tbsps (28ml) red wine vinegar

1 tsp Dijon mustard

1/2 tsp crushed garlic

Several grinds black pepper, to taste

170g mixed greens

1 medium tomato, sliced

35g crumbled blue cheese

The abundance of summer produce inspires many of my recipes. Here, cooking the vegetables with a smoker box on the barbecue adds a unique flavour to this salad. The blue cheese complements the flavours.

Preheat the barbecue to medium-high. Remove the ends from the crookneck squash and courgette and discard. Split the squash and scoop out the seeds, then slice lengthwise. Remove the end from the aubergine and discard. Slice the aubergine lengthwise. Place the squash and aubergine in a plastic bag and drizzle with the olive oil. Twist the bag to seal, allowing some air to remain in the bag. Toss gently to coat the vegetables evenly. Remove the squash and aubergine from the bag and place them on the barbecue. Barbecue for 8 to 10 minutes, turning frequently. Remove the squash and aubergine from the barbecue and place on a cutting board. Cool for several minutes, then cut into matchstick slices.

Meanwhile, place the extra-virgin olive oil, red wine vinegar, mustard, garlic, and black pepper in a bowl and whisk to combine.

Place the mixed greens in a large bowl and drizzle with half of the dressing, reserving the remaining dressing. Toss well to coat the leaves. Distribute the lettuce equally between 4 chilled salad plates. Arrange the tomato around the edge of each plate and place equal amounts of matchstick vegetable slices over the top. Drizzle with the remaining dressing. Top with the blue cheese and serve immediately.

Yield: 4 side-dish servings

Fresh Greens with
Barbecued Hearts of Palm

INGREDIENTS

220g tinned hearts of palm

1 tbsp (14ml) olive oil

2 tbsps (28ml) freshly squeezed
   lime juice

2 tsps finely chopped fresh oregano

225g loosely packed mixed salad
   greens

1 lemon cucumber, peeled and
   chopped

12 cherry tomatoes, halved

60ml extra-virgin olive oil

3 tsps finely chopped fresh flat-leaf
   parsley

1 tsp Dijon mustard

Pinch granulated garlic

You can find the ingredients to make this refreshing salad at any time of year. Hearts of palm are sold in tins in most supermarkets. The smaller stalks are always tender, but the larger ones can be a bit tough. If the tin you purchase has larger ones in it, peel away the outer layers before you marinate them.

Drain the hearts of palm and place in a shallow dish.

In a separate bowl, whisk together the olive oil, 1 tbsp of the lime juice, and 1 tsp of the oregano. Pour over the hearts of palm and marinate for about 15 minutes. Roll the hearts of palm to coat as they marinate.

Preheat the barbecue to medium-high. Meanwhile, place the greens in a medium bowl. Add the cucumber and tomatoes.

In a small bowl, whisk together the extra-virgin olive oil, the remaining 1 tbsp lime juice, the parsley, the remaining 1 tsp oregano, the mustard, and garlic to make a dressing. Set aside.

Place the hearts of palm in a barbecue basket on the barbecue and grill for about 5 minutes, turning frequently, until heated through and seared with barbecue marks. Remove from the barbecue to a cutting board and cut into thick slices. Toss the salad greens with the dressing and distribute equally between 4 salad plates. Top with equal amounts of barbecued hearts of palm and serve.

Yield: 4 side-dish servings

Red Lettuce Salad
with Barbecued Beets and Goats Cheese

INGREDIENTS

455g small fresh beets

75ml Raspberry Vinegar Marinade
(page 32)

170g loosely packed torn red lettuce leaves

3 tbsps (45ml) extra-virgin
olive oil

1 tbsp (14ml) raspberry vinegar

55g soft goats cheese

To make this beautiful and delicious salad, purchase small, fresh spring beets, measuring the weight with the tops removed. If you can find yellow beets, mix them with the red variety. The Raspberry Vinegar Marinade seasons the beets perfectly.

Peel the beets and cut them into $^1/_2$ cm slices. Place them in a bowl with the Raspberry Vinegar Marinade and toss to coat. Allow the beets to marinate for about 45 minutes, tossing occasionally.

Preheat the barbecue to medium. Place the beets on the barbecue and grill for about 15 minutes, turning several times, until fork-tender. Remove the beets from the barbecue to a cutting board. Cut the beets into strips and set aside to cool.

Meanwhile, place the lettuce in a shallow bowl.

In a small bowl, whisk together the olive oil and raspberry vinegar. Pour over the lettuce and toss to coat. Place equal amounts of lettuce on 4 serving plates. Arrange the beet strips on top and use a fork to crumble the goats cheese over the beets.

Yield: 4 side-dish servings

Spinach Salad with
Spiced Walnuts and Fire-Roasted Red Bell Pepper

INGREDIENTS

1 medium red bell pepper

180g loosely packed baby
spinach leaves

40g chopped raw,
unsalted walnuts

2 tsps freshly squeezed lime juice

1/4 tsp granulated garlic

1/4 tsp chilli powder

1/4 tsp salt

2 tbsps (28ml) orange juice

1 tbsp (14ml)
apple cider vinegar

1 tbsp (14ml
olive oil

1/2 small red onion, thinly sliced

Several grinds black pepper,
to taste

6 tsps finely chopped
fresh coriander

This composed salad is perfect for a fancy dinner, stunning in both visual appeal and flavour. The seasonings suggest Tex-Mex cuisine, so pair this with fajitas or quesadillas as the main course.

Preheat the barbecue to high. Place the bell pepper directly on the barbecue and cook for 10 to 15 minutes, turning frequently. Cook until the skin is charred black. Transfer the pepper to a plastic or paper bag, close the bag, and set aside for about 15 minutes. When the pepper is cool enough to handle, peel off the charred skin and discard the seeds, stem, and white membrane. Slice the pepper into thin 1-inch strips and set them aside.

Wash the spinach and discard the stems. Dry the spinach and coarsely tear into bite-size pieces. Place the spinach in a large bowl and set aside.

Heat a dry, heavy-bottomed frying pan over medium heat on the hob and toast the walnuts for about 5 minutes, shaking the pan frequently. When the walnuts are golden brown, place them in a small bowl and toss with the lime juice while they are still warm. Sprinkle on the garlic, chilli powder, and 1/8 tsp of the salt. Toss to distribute evenly and set aside.

Whisk together the orange juice, apple cider vinegar, vinegar, olive oil, and the remaining 1/8 tsp salt in a small bowl.

Toss together the spinach, onion, and orange juice mixture. Distribute evenly among 6 chilled salad plates. Top the spinach with the bell pepper strips and sprinkle with the spiced nuts. Grind a little black pepper on each one and sprinkle evenly with the coriander. Serve immediately.

Yield: 6 side-dish servings

Spinach Salad
with Barbecued Peaches and Gorgonzola Cheese

INGREDIENTS

3 tbsps (45ml)
extra-virgin olive oil

1 tbsp (14ml)
raspberry vinegar

1/4 tsp crushed garlic

Pinch salt

Several grinds black pepper, to taste

30g chopped pecans

180g loosely packed baby
spinach leaves

2 medium yellow peaches

28g crumbled Gorgonzola cheese

The sweet peaches and sharp Gorgonzola cheese go together well in this distinctive spinach salad.

Place the olive oil, raspberry vinegar, garlic, salt, and black pepper in a small bowl and whisk to combine into a dressing. Set aside.

Place the pecans in a small frying pan on the hob over medium-high heat. Shake the pan frequently until the pecans emit a roasted aroma. Remove the pecans from the pan and set aside until needed.

Wash the spinach and discard the stems. Dry the spinach and coarsely tear into bite-size pieces. Place the spinach in a shallow bowl and toss with the dressing just before serving.

When ready to serve, preheat the barbecue to medium-high. Cut each peach into 8 slices. Place the slices in a barbecue basket and put it on the barbecue. Barbecue for about 2 minutes, then turn and barbecue for about 2 more minutes.

Put equal portions of spinach on 4 salad plates. Top the spinach with peach slices, arranged around the perimeter of the plate. Sprinkle each salad with equal amounts of Gorgonzola cheese and pecans. Serve immediately.

Yield: 4 side-dish servings

Caesar Salad
with Smoky Barbecued Tofu

INGREDIENTS

400g extra-firm tofu

3 tbsps (45ml) olive oil

1 1/2 tbsps (21ml)
   balsamic vinegar

I large head romaine lettuce

I medium egg

2 cloves garlic, finely chopped

3 tbsps (45ml) freshly squeezed
   lemon juice

I tbsp (14ml)
   vegetarian Worcestershire sauce

120ml extra-virgin olive oil

30g croutons

50g finely grated Parmesan cheese

A good Caesar salad is hard to pass up, and this one, with barbecued tofu strips, is a delicious variation on this popular salad. The tofu is pressed to remove the water, then marinated briefly. Most of the oil that is used in the marinade drips off while barbecuing, producing a delightful flavour.

Preheat the barbecue to medium-high with a smoker box in place. Drain the tofu and cut the slab in half width-wise to create 2 pieces. Place each piece on a paper towel and cover with another towel. Place a heavy frying pan on top to press the excess water from the tofu. After 15 minutes, place the tofu between fresh paper towels and repeat the process.

In a bowl, whisk together the olive oil and balsamic vinegar and pour into a rimmed baking pan. Again, cut the tofu slabs in half width-wise and soak each side in the oil and vinegar mixture. Place the tofu on the hot barbecue. Barbecue for about 10 minutes, turning several times. Remove the tofu from the barbecue and set aside to cool slightly. When the tofu is cool enough to handle, cut into thin strips. Set aside.

Meanwhile, wash and dry the lettuce, then tear it into bite-size pieces, and briefly set it aside in the refrigerator to keep cold and crisp.

In a large bowl, whisk together the egg, garlic, lemon juice, and Worcestershire sauce. Gradually add the extra-virgin olive oil in a thin stream, whisking as you do. Continue to whisk for a minute or two until emulsified. Add the lettuce and toss well to coat with the dressing. Add the croutons and Parmesan cheese and toss again. Arrange equal amounts on chilled salad plates. Top with the strips of tofu and serve immediately.

Yield: 6 side-dish servings

Iceberg Lettuce
with Barbecued Figs and Creamy Blue Cheese Dressing

INGREDIENTS

175g mayonnaise

100g crumbled blue cheese

60g sour cream

2 tbsps (28ml) red wine vinegar

1 tbsp (12g) sugar

$^1/_2$ tsp crushed garlic

1 head iceberg lettuce

12 firm, ripe green figs

The crispness of the iceberg lettuce is perfect for this salad. The green figs with their purple-seeded centres soften as they barbecue and are delicious with the blue cheese dressing.

Place the mayonnaise, blue cheese, sour cream, red wine vinegar, sugar, and garlic in a bowl and whisk together to make the dressing. (There will be lumps of blue cheese in the creamy mixture.) Set aside in the refrigerator.

Remove the centre core from the lettuce and discard. Tear the rest into bite-size pieces, placing equal amounts of lettuce on 6 chilled salad plates. Set aside in the refrigerator.

Preheat the barbecue to medium-high. Cut off and discard the stem ends and slice the figs in half lengthwise. Place the figs cut sides up (skin sides down) on the barbecue and grill for about 4 minutes until the centres are soft. Remove the figs from the barbecue and arrange 4 halves on top of the lettuce on each plate. Spoon equal amounts of blue cheese dressing on each plate and serve immediately.

Yield: 6 side-dish servings

Barbecued Tomato Salad
with Fresh Mozzarella Cheese

INGREDIENTS

2 tomatoes

$1/2$ tsp mild chilli powder

$1/2$ tsp granulated garlic

2 balls fresh mozzarella
(about 225g)

2 tbsps (28ml) extra-virgin
olive oil

1 tsp balsamic vinegar

16 fresh basil leaves

$1/4$ tsp salt

Several grinds black pepper,
to taste

This salad is a twist on the classic Italian Insalata di Pomodoro e Mozzarella. *Look for fresh mozzarella cheese packed in water. It is sold at deli counters or speciality food markets.*

Preheat the barbecue to medium with a smoker box in place. Core the tomatoes and quarter them. Sprinkle the tomatoes with the chilli powder and the garlic. Place the tomatoes on the barbecue and barbecue for 2 to 3 minutes, then turn them and continue to barbecue for 2 to 3 minutes. Carefully remove the tomatoes from the barbecue and set aside.

Cut the mozzarella into 1cm slices. Arrange the barbecued tomato wedges on serving plates and place equal amounts of mozzarella slices on each plate. Drizzle with the olive oil, then with the balsamic vinegar.

Stack the basil leaves and cut them crosswise into thin strips. Distribute them on top of the tomato and cheese. Sprinkle with the salt and black pepper, then serve at room temperature.

Yield: 4 side-dish servings

Corn, Black Bean, and Avocado Salad

INGREDIENTS

60ml olive oil

60ml freshly squeezed
orange juice

3 tbsps (45ml) freshly squeezed
lime juice

1 tsp crushed garlic

$^1/_4$ tsp ground cumin

$^1/_2$ tsp salt

2 ears yellow corn, not husked

860g cooked black beans

2 Haas avocados, peeled, seeded,
and diced

240g peeled and diced jícama or
water chestnuts

6 spring onions, diced

8g chopped fresh coriander

The colours of this salad are a feast for the eyes, whetting the appetite for the first bite. Serve this as a side dish for a multi-course Tex-Mex theme dinner or as a main dish for 6 with tortilla chips and Guacamole (page 48). Haas avocados have pebbled deep green to black skin. This salad is best prepared ahead of time and refrigerated until needed.

To prepare the dressing, whisk together the olive oil, orange juice, lime juice, garlic, cumin, and salt in a small bowl. Set aside.

Place the corn in a plastic bag and fill the bag with water to soak the husks for about 15 minutes. Meanwhile, preheat the barbecue to high. Remove the corn from the bag of water and place the corn on the barbecue. Turn the corn every few minutes to evenly blacken all sides of the husks. Barbecue for 18 to 22 minutes. (The kernels will steam in the husks.) Remove the corn from the barbecue. Allow the corn to cool for a few minutes, then peel off the husks and remove the silk. Cut the corn from the cob and place in a large bowl.

Drain and rinse the black beans and add them to the corn. Toss in the avocado, jícama or water chestnuts, spring onions, and coriander. Drizzle with the dressing and toss. Refrigerate until needed.

Yield: 12 side-dish servings

Pasta Salad with
Barbecued Radicchio and Sweet Peppers

INGREDIENTS

1 head radicchio

1 small yellow bell pepper

1 small red bell pepper

2 tbsps (28ml
   olive oil

1 tsp crushed garlic

12 ounces (340g penne pasta

2 tbsps (28ml extra-virgin olive oil

1 tbsp (14ml balsamic vinegar

$1/8$ tsp mild chilli powder

2 tsps finely chopped fresh
   oregano

3 spring onions, finely chopped

Parmesan cheese (optional)

The colours in this salad will entice you before you and your guests even taste it. Radicchio is a member of the chicory family, and it is likely sold in the fresh greens section of your supermarket. This salad is easy to prepare and set aside in the refrigerator until you're ready to serve it.

Preheat the barbecue to medium. Cut the radicchio into quarters, removing the core section. Core and seed the bell peppers, cutting them into quarters. Place the radicchio and bell peppers in a plastic bag and drizzle with the olive oil and garlic. Twist the bag to seal, allowing some air to remain in the bag. Toss gently to coat the radicchio and peppers evenly.

Place the radicchio and peppers on the barbecue. Barbecue the radicchio for 5 to 7 minutes, turning carefully to slightly char all sides. Barbecue the peppers until limp and slightly charred, 6 to 7 minutes. Remove the radicchio and peppers from the barbecue and coarsely chop.

Meanwhile, fill a large stockpot with water and place on the hob over high heat. Bring to a boil and add the pasta. Cook for 6 to 8 minutes, until al dente. Drain into a colander and rinse with cold water. Drain well and transfer to a shallow serving bowl.

In a bowl, whisk together the extra-virgin olive oil, balsamic vinegar, chilli powder, and oregano. Drizzle over the pasta and toss to coat. Add the spring onions and the barbecueed radicchio and peppers, toss to combine, and serve. Pass grated Parmesan cheese, if desired.

Yield: 8 side-dish servings

Pasta Salad with
Barbecued Vegetables and Garlic-Chipotle Dressing

INGREDIENTS

2 medium bulbs garlic

3 tbsps (45ml) plus $^1/_4$ tsp olive oil

2 medium yellow onions

1 medium aubergine

3 tsps coarse salt

3 medium courgette

12 ounces (340g)
   spiral-shaped pasta

6 tbsps (90ml) freshly squeezed
   lime juice

6 tsps finely chopped chipotle
   chillies in adobo

$^1/_2$ tsp salt

60ml extra-virgin olive oil

170g crumbled queso fresco or
   ricotta cheese

This slightly spicy, slightly smoky pasta salad is a summertime favourite. The flavours intermingle to create a Tex-Mex dish. The chipotle chillies in adobo are available in ethnic food shops, on the internet at www.coolchile.co.uk, or you can experiment by substituting chipotle ketchup or ready-made chipotle dressing.

Preheat the barbecue to medium. Rub the papery skin from the garlic, but do not break them into individual cloves. Cut about 1cm off the pointed top ends of the bulbs and rub the cut surfaces with $^1/_4$ tsp of the olive oil. Place the garlic bulbs cut side up in a covered clay or glass baking dish and place on the barbecue. (You could wrap the garlic in foil. Then place the foil packet on a baking stone or on baking bricks so the garlic cooks but does not burn on the bottom.) Barbecue for about 45 minutes. When the garlic feel very soft when gently squeezed, remove the garlic from the foil or garlic baker so it can cool.

Meanwhile, trim the ends from the onions and peel them. Cut the onions in half crosswise and lightly brush the cut sides with some of the remaining olive oil. Place the onions on the barbecue cut sides down and barbecue for 35 to 45 minutes, turning every 8 to 10 minutes to cook evenly. When the onions are soft and slightly charred, remove from the barbecue and set aside.

Cut off and discard the stem and bottom ends of the aubergine, but do not peel it. Cut the aubergine crosswise into 1cm slices. To remove the aubergine's bitter juices, sprinkle both sides of the slices with the salt and place on a rack for about 30 minutes. (The salt will cause the aubergine to 'sweat' and release the bitter juices.) Briefly rinse the aubergine slices and blot them dry with kitchen paper. Brush each side of the aubergine slices with some of the remaining olive oil and place them on the barbecue. Barbecue for

5 to 8 minutes until lightly browned, then turn and continue to barbecue for another 5 to 8 minutes. (The slices should be tender-crisp, not mushy.)

While you are preparing the aubergine, trim off and discard the ends of the courgette and cut the courgette in thirds lengthwise. Lightly brush the cut sides with some of the remaining olive oil. Place the courgette on the barbecue and barbecue for 4 to 6 minutes, watching closely and turning frequently. Remove the courgette from the barbecue and cool slightly. Coarsely chop the onions, aubergine, and courgette and place in a large bowl.

Meanwhile, bring several quarts of water to a boil in a large stock pot on the hob. Cook the pasta for 6 to 8 minutes until al dente and pour into a large colander. Rinse with cold water and drain well. Transfer the pasta to the bowl with the vegetables and toss to combine.

Squeeze the barbecued garlic paste into a blender. Add the lime juice, chipotle chillies, and salt. With the machine running, pour the extra-virgin olive oil into the blender and puree. Pour over the vegetables and pasta and toss to combine. Sprinkle on chunks of the queso fresco and toss again. Serve immediately or refrigerate for several hours. Bring to room temperature before serving.

Yield: 10 side-dish servings

Asparagus
with Watercress Sauce

This dish signals spring has finally arrived! Choose the thickest asparagus stalks you can because they're the most succulent and will produce the best results.

INGREDIENTS

3 tbsps (45ml) extra-virgin olive oil

2 tbsps (28ml) freshly squeezed lemon juice

$1/8$ tsp salt

17g watercress leaves

2 spring onions, finely chopped

1kg fresh asparagus

1 tbsp (14ml) olive oil

1 hard-boiled egg, peeled and chopped

Combine the extra-virgin olive oil, lemon juice, and salt in a small bowl.

Place the watercress and onions in a blender. Switch on the low setting and add the lemon juice mixture in a slow, steady stream. Blend until you have a smooth sauce. Set aside.

Preheat the barbecue to medium. Wash the asparagus carefully to remove any traces of soil. Snap off and discard the tough ends. Place the asparagus in a plastic bag and drizzle with the olive oil. Twist the bag to seal, allowing some of the air to remain in the bag. Toss gently to coat the asparagus evenly. Place the asparagus in a barbecue basket on the barbecue. Barbecue for 8 to 10 minutes, turning frequently so the stalks cook but do not burn. (The asparagus should be al dente and slightly charred.) Remove the asparagus from the barbecue to a serving platter. Spoon the watercress sauce over the top and sprinkle with the chopped egg. Serve hot or at room temperature.

Yield: 10 side-dish servings

Baby Bok Choy
with Lemon Miso Sauce

Use small, tender bok choy, usually available from Asian food markets.

INGREDIENTS

60ml freshly squeezed lemon juice

2 tbsps (35g white miso

2 cloves garlic, finely chopped

3 tsps cornstarch

455g baby bok choy

2 tbsps (28ml) toasted sesame oil

Preheat the barbecue to medium-high. In a small saucepan, whisk together the lemon juice, miso, garlic, and 60ml water. Place on the hob over low heat and cook until steaming.

Place 2 tbsps (28ml) water in a small jar with a tight-fitting lid and add the cornstarch. Cover tightly and shake to dissolve. Whisk the cornstarch mixture into the saucepan and cook over medium-low heat until thickened, about 1 minute. (Do not overcook or it will get gummy.) Remove the saucepan from the heat and set aside in a warm spot.

Rinse the bok choy and shake to remove some of the water. Cut any larger heads in half lengthwise. Place the bok choy in a plastic bag and drizzle with the sesame oil. Twist the bag to seal, allowing some air to remain in the bag. Toss gently to coat the bok choy evenly. Place the bok choy on the barbecue and barbecue for 3 to 5 minutes, turning frequently, until the leaves are limp and slightly charred. Remove the bok choy from the barbecue and place on a serving platter. Drizzle with the sauce and serve immediately.

Yield: 6 side-dish servings

Summer Squashes
with Lemon Basil

INGREDIENTS

I large butternut squash

3 medium courgette

2 tbsps (28ml
   olive oil

I tsp crushed garlic

I tbsp (14ml
   extra-virgin olive oil

I tbsp chiffonaded strips fresh
   lemon basil (see page 16 for this
   technique)

Lemon basil is one of the many varieties that are easy to grow in the summer garden. You may use any type of fresh basil, but I think lemon basil imparts the best flavour to this dish. You could use an assortment of summer squashes to create a colourful platter of barbecued vegetables.

Preheat the barbecue to medium. Split the squash and scoop out the seeds. Remove and discard the stem ends of the squash and courgette, and then cut them lengthwise into 1cm slices. Place the squash and courgette in a plastic bag and drizzle with the olive oil and garlic. Twist the bag to seal, allowing some of the air to remain in the bag. Toss gently to coat the squash and courgette evenly. Place the squash and courgette on the barbecue and barbecue for about 10 minutes, until barbecue marks appear and the slices are tender-crisp, turning twice. Remove the squashes and courgette and place on a platter. Drizzle with the extra-virgin olive oil and sprinkle with the lemon basil. Serve immediately or at room temperature.

Yield: 6 side-dish servings

BBQ Courgettes

Choose small courgettes for this classic summer side dish to avoid the watery seed pockets that develop in the larger ones.

INGREDIENTS

6 small courgettes

1 1/2 tbsps (21ml) olive oil

1 tsp crushed garlic

1 tbsp (14ml)
  balsamic vinegar

1/8 tsp salt

Several grinds black pepper,
  to taste

Preheat the barbecue to medium. Remove and discard the stem ends of the courgettes and cut lengthwise into 1cm slices. Place the courgettes in a plastic bag and drizzle with the olive oil and garlic. Twist the bag to seal, allowing some of the air to remain in the bag. Toss gently to coat the courgettes evenly.

Place the courgettes on the barbecue and grill for about 10 minutes until tender-crisp, turning two to three times. Remove the courgettes from the barbecue to a serving plate. Drizzle with the balsamic vinegar and sprinkle with the salt and black pepper. Serve immediately.

Yield: 4 side-dish servings

Barbecued Onions
with Red Wine Vinaigrette

This recipe uses yellow onions because they are available year-round. Early in the season, try this dish with fresh spring torpedo-shaped onions for a delightful variation.

INGREDIENTS

4 small yellow onions

1 tbsp (14ml) olive oil

2 tbsps (28ml) extra-virgin olive oil

1 tbsp (14ml) red wine vinegar

1 tbsp (14ml) freshly squeezed
  lemon juice

1/2 tsp crushed garlic

Pinch cayenne

1 small loaf country bread, sliced

Preheat the barbecue to medium-high. Trim off and discard the ends of the onions and peel them. Cut the onions in half across the middle. Rub equal amounts of the olive oil over the cut sides. Place the onions, cut sides down, directly on the barbecue. Cover the barbecue and grill for about 45 minutes, turning every 10 to 12 minutes. (The onions are done when they are soft and slightly charred.)

Meanwhile, whisk together the extra-virgin olive oil, red wine vinegar, lemon juice, garlic, and cayenne in a small bowl. Place the onions on a serving plate and drizzle with the olive oil mixture. Serve immediately, passing the bread.

Yield: 4 side-dish servings

White Corn
with Chilli Butter

Choose ears of corn that are fully encased by their husks, with the light-coloured silk intact. Watch the barbecue carefully as the corn cooks because it needs to be turned frequently. The results are delicious!

INGREDIENTS

6 ears white corn, not husked

2 tbsps (28g) butter

$^1/_2$ tsp crushed garlic

$^1/_4$ tsp chilli powder

Pinch salt

Place the corn in a plastic bag and fill the bag with water to soak the husks for about 15 minutes.

Meanwhile, preheat the barbecue to high. Place the butter in a small dish and melt in the microwave. Add the garlic, chilli powder, and salt and heat for several seconds. Set aside.

Remove the corn from the bag of water and place the corn on the barbecue. Turn every few minutes to evenly blacken all sides of the husks. Barbecue for 18 to 22 minutes. (The kernels will steam in the husks.) Remove the corn from the barbecue. Allow the corn to cool for a few minutes, then peel off the husks and remove the silk. Place the corn on a serving platter. Brush with the chilli butter and serve immediately.

Yield: 6 side-dish servings

Barbecued Red Potatoes

INGREDIENTS

6 red potatoes

2 tbsps (28ml)
   olive oil

$^1/_2$ tsp crushed garlic

$^1/_8$ tsp salt

Easy to prepare, these potatoes are great with a skewered entrée and a dipping sauce. Try with the Dilled Yogurt and Sour Cream Sauce (page 51).

Preheat the barbecue to medium-high. Scrub the potatoes but do not peel them. Place the potatoes in the microwave oven and cook on high for 4 minutes, until slightly soft. Let the potatoes cool for a few minutes, then cut in half. Place the potatoes in a plastic bag and drizzle with the olive oil and garlic, then sprinkle with the salt. Twist the bag to seal, allowing some of the air to remain in the bag. Toss gently to coat the potatoes evenly. Remove the potatoes from the bag, place on the barbecue, and barbecue for 5 minutes. Turn the potatoes and continue to barbecue for 5 more minutes. Turn the potatoes again and barbecue for about 5 additional minutes on each side, until the potatoes are fork-tender and lightly browned. Serve immediately.

Yield: 6 side-dish servings

Barbecued Sweet Potatoes

INGREDIENTS

4 medium red-skinned
   sweet potatoes

2 tbsps (28ml)
   olive oil

$^1/_2$ tsp granulated garlic

60g low-fat sour cream

$^1/_4$ tsp paprika

Have you ever wondered what to do with sweet potatoes during the summertime? Barbecuing them is the answer! Serve them hot with barbecued skewered entrées or as a finger-food appetizer while you prepare the rest of the meal.

Preheat the barbecue to medium-high. Scrub the sweet potatoes, but do not peel them. Slice the potatoes crosswise into 1cm rounds. Place the potatoes in a plastic bag and drizzle with the olive oil, then sprinkle with the garlic. Twist the bag to seal, allowing some air to remain in the bag. Toss gently to coat the sweet potatoes evenly. Remove the potatoes from the bag and place on the barbecue. Barbecue for 10 to 12 minutes, turning frequently, until fork-tender and showing barbecue marks. Remove the potatoes from the barbecue and arrange on a large warm platter. Spoon a small amount of sour cream on top of each sweet-potato round. Sprinkle with the paprika and serve immediately.

Yield: 6 side-dish servings

Aussie Chips with Sweet Chilli Sauce

INGREDIENTS

4 russet potatoes

60ml canola oil

I tsp crushed garlic

$^1/_2$ tsp salt

60ml sweet chilli sauce

60g Mexican Crema (page 54)

My friends Candy and Al Holland's daughter, Gill, spent a semester as an exchange student in Australia. Upon her return, she raved about potatoes cooked on the barbecue served with a chilli sauce. These chips are cooked on the barbecue and served with a prepared chilli sauce that you can easily find in Asian markets.

Preheat the barbecue to medium-high. Scrub the potatoes, but do not peel them. Cut the potatoes lengthwise into chunky chips.

In a small bowl, whisk together the canola oil, garlic, and salt. Place the potatoes in a plastic bag and drizzle with the oil mixture. Twist the bag to seal, allowing some air to remain in the bag. Toss gently to coat the potatoes evenly.

Place the potatoes on the barbecue and grill for 12 to 16 minutes, turning frequently, until they are crisp on the outside and tender but moist on the inside. Transfer the potatoes to a serving plate.

Place the sweet chilli sauce and Mexican Crema in small dipping bowls. Pass the potatoes, allowing diners to dip in the sauces as desired.

Yield: 8 side-dish servings

Russet Potato Wedges

Everyone loves baked potatoes, and these barbecued wedges are a flavourful twist on that side dish. Serve with sour cream or Creamy Horseradish Sauce (page 59).

INGREDIENTS

4 medium russet potatoes

2 tbsps (28ml) olive oil

$1/2$ tsp paprika

$1/4$ tsp salt

Preheat the barbecue to medium-high. Scrub the potatoes but do not peel. Cut the potatoes lengthwise into wedges and place in a plastic bag. Drizzle with the olive oil and sprinkle with the paprika and salt. Twist the bag to seal, allowing some of the air to remain in the bag. Toss gently to coat the potatoes evenly.

Place the potatoes on the barbecue and cook for about 15 minutes, turning frequently. (The potatoes should be fork-tender but not falling apart.) Transfer the potatoes to a serving plate and serve immediately.

Yield: 6 side-dish servings

CHAPTER 6

Pizza and en Papillote Entrées

Turning your barbecue into a pizza oven is simple – just add a baking stone to the barbecue as you heat it. Then quickly transfer the pizza from a baker's paddle to the baking stone on the barbecue and cook it – it's that easy! You may also cook the pizza on a ceramic pizza plate, preheated on the barbecue. The baking stone and ceramic pizza plate both produce a crisp crust and evenly cooked pizza. Be sure to sprinkle the cooking surface with cornmeal.

Prepare a fresh crust from the Basic Pizza Crust recipe on page 105 or use a commercially prepared crust. Once you've prepared the crust, the pizza comes together quickly, so be sure to have all of your ingredients chopped up, measured, and at hand, so you can place them on top of the crust and transfer it quickly to the barbecue.

Some of the pizza recipes I've included are on the light side, while others are more substantial. Choose salad and side dishes to accompany them depending on your diners' appetites. Pair the Pesto Pizza (page 107) or the Asparagus Pizza (page 108) with a leafy salad that is sprinkled with goat cheese for a delightful light supper. For a more hearty meal, serve the Pizza with Barbecued Aubergine, Garlic, and Mozzarella (page 110) along with steamed green beans and a fresh tomato salad.

To prepare and present a fancy *en papillote* dish, you only need to master one simple technique. Tightly wrapped in kitchen parchment paper or heavy foil, the ingredients are tender, moist, and infused with flavour. The paper packets are easy to assemble and fun to serve.

How to Make and Assemble en Papillote Packets

To make greaseproof-paper packets, use a piece of greaseproof paper about 45 x 50cm for each serving. Fold each piece in half to create rectangles. Use scissors to cut each rectangle into a half-heart shape. Open out the hearts and distribute equal amounts of the ingredients, positioning them near the centre of each crease. Add any spices or liquids to each packet. Close the heart so that the edges of the paper meet. Beginning at the round end, fold over about 1.5cm of the paper and crease sharply. Work your way around the shape of the heart, folding in the edges and creasing sharply in overlapping pleats. Twist the pointy end to seal everything tightly in the packet. Repeat this process with the remaining packets.

For heavy-duty foil packets, use a 35 x 50cm piece of foil for each packet. Place the foil on a work surface, creasing it lengthwise in the centre. Mound the ingredients on one side of the crease. Add any spices or liquids to each packet. Fold the other section of the foil over the ingredients. Crimp the side sections to seal. You can do a fancy presentation by forming the remaining narrow end into a 'swan's neck' by twisting it and forming an 'S' shape. Crimp the bottom to form a 'tail'.

When you're ready to cook, place the packets in a single layer on a baking stone and barbecue for about 15 minutes. I like to remove the packets from the barbecue directly to the serving plate and allow the diners to open their packets, releasing the aromas that have built up inside. The Curried Cauliflower and Carrots *en Papillote* (page 115) and the Asparagus, Shiitake Mushrooms and Tofu *en Papillote* (page 117) are particularly aromatic.

The *en papillote* packets may be prepared ahead of time and refrigerated until you are ready to put them on the barbecue. Add a couple of minutes to the cooking time because the ingredients will be cold. These recipes are easy to double, so they are wonderful to prepare for a dinner party.

Basic Pizza Crust

INGREDIENTS

7g active dry yeast (1 envelope)

355ml lukewarm water
(105° to 115°F)

2 tbsps (28ml) plus $^{1}/_{2}$ tsp olive oil

$^{1}/_{2}$ tsp salt

440 to 500g unbleached
white flour

Use bread flour or unbleached white flour. The flour measure is given as a range because the exact amount of flour will vary depending on the day's humidity and other weather conditions. The temperature of the water to start the yeast is important — too hot, and it will kill the yeast; too cold, and the yeast will not activate. Use an instant-read thermometer to make sure the water temperature is in the 105° to 115°F range.

Place the yeast in a large warm bowl and add the lukewarm water. Stir the mixture with a wooden spoon to dissolve the yeast, then set aside in a warm place until creamy in appearance, about 15 minutes. Stir in 2 tbsps of the olive oil and the salt, and then add half of the flour. Stir to incorporate, using a large wooden spoon. (The mixture will be very sticky at this point.) Add anothr quarter of the flour and continue to stir until the dough begins to form a ball. Turn the dough out onto a lightly floured work surface and knead until it is soft and smooth, about 10 minutes, adding the remaining flour as needed, a bit at a time, until the dough is no longer sticky. If necessary, add up to 6og more flour, a tbsp at a

continued on next page >

Basic Pizza Crust, continued

time. (Too much flour will result in a dry dough that will produce a slightly tough crust.)

Lightly oil a large bowl with the remaining $^1/_2$ tsp oil. Place the dough ball in the oiled bowl, turn it to coat the entire surface with oil, and cover the bowl with a clean dish towel. Place the bowl in a warm, draft-free place for the dough to rise until doubled in volume, about $1^1/_2$ hours.

After the dough has risen, punch it down with your fist to press out most of the air.

Place the dough on a lightly floured work surface and divide it into 2 balls of equal size. Working with 1 ball at a time, flatten the dough with your hands into a circle about 12cm in diameter and 3cm thick. Begin working from the centre, pressing the dough outward with the heels of your hands. (If the dough sticks to your hands, sprinkle it lightly with flour.) Push the dough into a 30cm round that is slightly thicker at the edges. (You can also use a rolling pin to press the dough into a 30cm round.)

If you are only making one pizza, wrap the remaining dough ball tightly and freeze it for up to 3 months. Thaw the dough at room temperature for a few hours before rolling out as directed above. Proceed with the instructions for the individual recipes.

Yield: two 12-inch pizza crusts

Pesto Pizza

INGREDIENTS

1 pizza crust (30cm in
diameter)

2 tbsps (17g
cornmeal

60g prepared marinara sauce

150g coarsely grated
mozzarella cheese

1 tbsp (14ml) olive oil

200g Basil Pesto (page 27)

One of the joys of having a summer garden is growing fresh basil to turn into pesto! It only takes a couple of plants to produce abundant harvests – and you can grow interesting varieties like lemon basil that can be hard to find in the super-market. You can also use commercially prepared pesto in this recipe. This pizza is heaven on a warm summer day.

Prepare the Basic Pizza Crust (page 105) or use a commercially prepared crust. Place a baking stone or ceramic pizza plate on the barbecue and preheat the barbecue to high.

Place the uncooked crust on a baker's paddle or rimless baking sheet that is well dusted with the cornmeal. Spread the marinara sauce evenly over the uncooked crust, leaving a 3cm rim. Sprinkle the mozzarella cheese evenly over the sauce. Brush the rim of the uncooked crust with the olive oil.

Transfer the pizza to the baking stone on the barbecue. Bake for 15 to 20 minutes, until the crust is crisp and the cheese has melted. Remove the pizza from the barbecue and drizzle with the Basil Pesto. Cut the pizza into 8 slices and serve immediately.

Yield: 2 main-dish servings or 4 side-dish servings

Asparagus Pizza

This pizza is light and flavourful. Serve it for dinner with a big salad or as part of a luncheon party.

INGREDIENTS

1 bulb garlic

2 ¼ tsps olive oil

1 pizza crust (30cm in diameter)

8 medium-thick stalks asparagus

2 tbsps (17g) cornmeal

130g coarsely grated Fontina
   cheese

25g chopped
   kalamata olives

55g crumbled soft goats cheese

Preheat the barbecue to medium. Rub the papery skin from the garlic, but do not break into individual cloves. Cut about 1cm off the pointed top end of the bulb and rub the surface with ¼ tsp of the olive oil. Place the garlic bulb, cut side up, in a covered clay or glass baking dish and place on the barbecue. (You could wrap the garlic in foil. Then place the foil packet on a baking stone or on baking bricks so the garlic cooks but does not burn on the bottom.) Barbecue for about 45 minutes. When the garlic feels very soft when gently squeezed, remove from the barbecue and uncover to cool. When the garlic is cool enough to handle, squeeze the garlic from the individual cloves into a small bowl and set aside.

Prepare the Basic Pizza Crust (page 105) or use a commercially prepared crust.

Snap off and discard the tough ends from the asparagus and cut the stems at a slant into 3cm pieces. Place the asparagus in a plastic bag and drizzle with 1 tsp of the olive oil. Twist the bag to seal, allowing some of the air to remain in the bag. Toss gently to coat the asparagus evenly. Remove the asparagus from the bag. Place a barbecue basket on the barbecue and evenly distribute the asparagus in the basket. Barbecue for 5 to 6 minutes, turning frequently. Remove the asparagus and barbecue basket, and set aside. Place the baking stone or ceramic pizza plate on the barbecue and increase the barbecue temperature to high.

Place the uncooked crust on a baker's paddle or rimless baking sheet that is well dusted with the cornmeal. Evenly sprinkle the Fontina cheese over the crust, leaving a 3cm rim. Use a rubber spatula to spread the garlic over the crust, distributing it evenly with the cheese. Top with the asparagus and kalamata olives. Crumble the goats cheese over the pizza. Brush the rim of the crust with the remaining 1 tsp olive oil.

Transfer the pizza to the baking stone or ceramic pizza plate on the barbecue. Bake for 15 to 20 minutes, until the crust is crisp and the cheese has melted. Remove from the barbecue and cut into 8 slices. Serve immediately.

Yield: 4 main-dish servings

Asparagus and Mushroom Pizza
with Mustard, Dill, Mozzarella, and Feta

INGREDIENTS

1 pizza crust (30cm in diameter)

2 tbsps (17g)
   cornmeal

455g asparagus

225g button mushrooms, sliced

3 cloves garlic, finely chopped

1/8 tsp salt

Several grinds black pepper,
   to taste

2 tbsps (30g) whole grain
   mustard

40g thinly sliced red onion

115g grated mozzarella cheese

28g crumbled feta cheese

3 tsps finely chopped fresh dill

1/4 tsp paprika

Asparagus is a springtime treat, and this innovative pizza is just one more way to enjoy this succulent vegetable.

Prepare the Basic Pizza Crust (page 105) or use a commercially prepared crust. Place a baking stone or ceramic pizza plate on the barbecue and preheat the barbecue to high. Place the uncooked crust on a baker's paddle or rimless baking sheet that is well dusted with the cornmeal. Set aside.

Rinse the asparagus. Break off and discard the tough ends. Slice the asparagus at a slant into 3cm pieces. Place the asparagus in a frying pan on the hob with the mushrooms, garlic, salt, black pepper, and 2 tbsps (28ml) water. Cover and cook over medium heat for 5 minutes, then remove the lid and continue to cook for about 5 minutes, stirring frequently. (Most of the liquid should have evaporated.)

Meanwhile, use a rubber spatula to spread the mustard over the pizza crust, leaving a 3cm rim around the outside. Use a slotted spoon to transfer the asparagus mixture to the pizza, spreading it out evenly and leaving a 3cm rim around the outer edge. Distribute the onion slices evenly over the asparagus mixture, and then top with the mozzarella cheese. Sprinkle the feta cheese and dill over the mozzarella cheese, and then dust with the paprika.

Transfer the pizza to the baking stone or ceramic pizza plate on the barbecue. Bake for 15 to 20 minutes, until the crust is crisp and the cheese has softened and browned a bit. Remove the pizza from the barbecue and cut into 8 wedges. Serve immediately.

Yield: 4 main-dish servings

Pizza with Garlic Tomato Sauce, Ricotta, and Fresh Greens

INGREDIENTS

1 pizza crust (30cm in diameter)

2 tbsps (17g cornmeal

3 pear tomatoes

2 tbsps (35g)
   tomato paste

2 cloves garlic, finely chopped

6 tsps finely grated Parmesan
   cheese

25g chopped kalamata olives

125g part-skim ricotta cheese

2 tbsps (30g)
   low-fat sour cream

1 tsp dried oregano

1 tbsp (14ml)
   olive oil

1 tsp lemon juice

$1/8$ tsp salt

Several grinds black pepper,
   to taste

40g mixed baby salad greens

This pizza is salad and entrée all in one! Prepare it for a lovely lunch or light supper.

Prepare the Basic Pizza Crust (page 105) or use a commercially prepared crust. Place a baking stone or ceramic pizza plate on the barbecue and preheat the barbecue to high. Place the uncooked crust on a baker's paddle or rimless baking sheet that is well dusted with the cornmeal.

Without peeling them, cut the tomatoes into quarters and place them in a blender. Add the tomato paste and garlic, then puree until smooth and set aside.

Sprinkle the Parmesan cheese evenly over the crust, then evenly top with the pureed tomatoes, leaving a 3cm border free of sauce. Distribute the kalamata olives on top of the sauce.

In a bowl, combine the ricotta cheese, sour cream, and $1/2$ tsp of the oregano. Place 8 heaping tbsps of the mixture on the pizza, within the ring of sauce and extending toward its outer edge. Crumble the remaining $1/2$ tsp oregano over the pizza. Transfer the pizza to the baking stone or ceramic pizza plate on the barbecue. Bake for 15 to 20 minutes, until the crust is crisp and the cheese has softened and browned a bit.

Meanwhile, in a small bowl, whisk together the olive oil, lemon juice, salt, and black pepper. Place the greens in a bowl and drizzle with the dressing. Remove the pizza from the barbecue and cut into 8 wedges. Mound the greens in the centre of the pizza and serve immediately.

Yield: 4 main-dish servings

Pizza with BBQ Aubergine, Garlic, and Mozzarella

INGREDIENTS

1 pizza crust (30cm in diameter)

1 bulb garlic

2 tbsps (28ml)
   plus 1 1/4 tsps olive oil

1 medium aubergine

2 tbsps (17g)
   cornmeal

60ml Tomato Coulis (page 24)

6 ounces (170g grated
   mozzarella cheese

1/4 tsp dried oregano

1/8 tsps salt

Several grinds black pepper,
   to taste

This pizza is the perfect summer entrée when the garden yields fresh, sweet tomatoes and tender aubergine. Prepare the Tomato Coulis in advance so everything is ready when you begin to prepare the pizza.

Prepare the Basic Pizza Crust (page 105) or use a commercially prepared crust. Preheat the barbecue to medium. Rub the papery skin from the garlic, but do not break into individual cloves. Cut about 1cm off the pointed top end of the bulb and rub the cut surface with 1/4 tsp of the olive oil. Place the garlic bulb, cut side up, in a covered clay or glass baking dish and place on the barbecue. (You can wrap it in foil. Then place the foil packet on a baking stone or on baking bricks so the garlic cooks but does not burn on the bottom.) Barbecue for about 45 minutes. When the garlic feels very soft when gently squeezed, remove from the barbecue and uncover to cool.

Remove and discard the stem of the aubergine, but do not peel. Cut the aubergine lengthwise into 1cm slices. Brush one side of the aubergine slices with 1 tbsp of the olive oil and place the aubergine oiled sides down on the barbecue. Grill for 4 to 6 minutes. Brush the top side of the aubergine with 1 tbsp of the oil and turn. Continue to barbecue for 4 to 6 minutes. Remove from the barbecue and set aside.

Place a baking stone or ceramic pizza plate on the barbecue and increase the barbecue temperature to high.

Place the uncooked pizza crust on a baker's paddle or a rimless baking sheet that is well dusted with the cornmeal. Press the garlic from the skins into a small bowl and spread evenly over the crust. Spread the Tomato Coulis over the garlic on the pizza crust. Distribute half of the mozzarella cheese evenly over the tomato sauce and then arrange the aubergine slices evenly over that in a fan pattern. Distribute the remaining cheese over the aubergine. Drizzle the outer edge of the pizza with the remaining tsp of olive oil. Sprinkle the pizza with the oregano, salt, and black pepper.

Transfer the pizza to the baking stone on the barbecue. Bake for 15 to 20 minutes, until the crust is crisp and the cheese is melted. Remove the pizza from the barbecue and cut into 8 wedges. Serve immediately.

Yield: 4 main-dish servings

Pizza with Courgette, Artichokes, and Feta Cheese

Create flavours of the Mediterranean in your own back garden.

INGREDIENTS

1 pizza crust (30cm in diameter)

2 tbsps (17g)
cornmeal

400g tinned water-packed
artichoke hearts

1 medium courgette

55g thinly sliced Provolone cheese

$\frac{1}{2}$ small red onion, thinly sliced

6 tsps finely chopped fresh
oregano

55g crumbled feta cheese

Several grinds black pepper,
to taste

Prepare the Basic Pizza Crust (page 105) or use a commercially prepared crust. Place a baking stone or ceramic pizza plate on the barbecue and preheat the barbecue to high. Place the uncooked crust on a baker's paddle or rimless baking sheet that is well dusted with the cornmeal.

Drain the artichoke hearts and coarsely chop them. Remove and discard the ends of the courgette and cut it into very thin oblong slices. Distribute the Provolone slices so that they cover most of the pizza crust, leaving a 3cm border. Arrange the onion over the top of the Provolone cheese, then place the courgette and artichoke hearts on top of the onion. Distribute the oregano and the feta cheese over the top and grind on the black pepper.

Transfer the pizza to the baking stone or ceramic pizza plate on the barbecue. Bake for 15 to 20 minutes, until the crust is crisp and the cheese has melted. Cut into 8 wedges and serve immediately.

Yield: 4 main-dish servings

BBQ Pepper and Chard Pizza
with Cumin, Jalapeños, and Coriander

INGREDIENTS

I pizza crust (30cm in diameter)

I large red bell pepper

455g Swiss chard

I tbsp (14ml) olive oil

I small onion, diced

6 cloves garlic, finely chopped

I 1/2 tsps cumin seed

Scant 1/8 tsp salt

2 tbsps (17g) cornmeal

55g grated Cheddar cheese

25g finely grated Parmesan cheese

3 tsps finely chopped pickled
    jalapeño chillies

6 tsps finely chopped
    fresh coriander

A spicy delight, this dish combines some classic Tex-Mex flavours on a pizza crust.

Prepare the Basic Pizza Crust (page 105) or use a commercially prepared one. Preheat the barbecue to high. Place the bell pepper directly on the barbecue and barbecue for 10 to 15 minutes, turning frequently. (The skin will be charred black.) Transfer the pepper to a plastic or paper bag, close the bag, and set aside for 15 minutes. When the pepper is cool enough to handle, peel off the skin and discard the stem, seeds, and white membrane. Thinly slice the pepper and set aside.

Wash the chard leaves, but do not dry them. Thinly slice the stems and coarsely chop the leaves; set the stems and leaves aside separately.

Heat the olive oil in a frying pan over medium heat. Add the onion, garlic, cumin, and salt and sauté for a moment, then stir in the chard stems and salt. Sauté for 5 minutes, then mound the greens on top, cover tightly, and cook an additional 5 minutes. (The greens should be wilted.) Stir to combine them with the other ingredients in the pan. Continue to cook for a minute or two, stirring constantly, until all the liquid has evaporated. Remove from the heat.

Place a baking stone or ceramic pizza plate on the barbecue.

Place the uncooked crust on a baker's paddle or rimless baking sheet that is well dusted with the cornmeal. Distribute the cooked greens evenly over the pizza crust and arrange the pepper slices on top of them in a pretty pattern.

In a small bowl, toss together the Cheddar cheese, Parmesan cheese, jalapeño chillies, and coriander. Distribute evenly over the pizza. Transfer the pizza to the baking stone or ceramic pizza plate on the barbecue. Bake for 15 to 20 minutes, until the crust is crisp and the cheese has melted. Remove from the barbecue and cut into 8 slices. Serve immediately.

Yield: 4 main-dish servings

Individual Pizzas
with Tomatoes, Feta, and Kalamata Olives

INGREDIENTS

2 medium plum tomatoes, diced

10g chopped fresh basil

2 tbsps (15g) capers, drained

Several grinds black pepper,
   to taste

4 whole-wheat pita breads or
   Middle Eastern flat breads

60ml olive oil

50g chopped kalamata olives

4 spring onions, diced

170g crumbled feta

This is a fabulous and quick summer dinner to prepare. The individual pizzas can be customized to each diner's taste, or all prepared the same way. As the pizzas barbecue, the feta cheese does not melt, but it becomes soft as all of the ingredients heat through.

Place the tomatoes in a bowl and add the basil, capers, and black pepper. Set aside.

Preheat the barbecue to medium. Brush one side of each pita bread or flat bread with some of the olive oil and place on the barbecue, oiled sides down, for 1 to 2 minutes. Remove the pitas from the barbecue to a baker's paddle or rimless baking sheet and brush the other sides with olive oil. Turn the pitas over and top the barbecued sides with equal amounts of the tomato mixture, olives, spring onions, and feta cheese.

Place the pitas back on the barbecue, oiled sides down, and barbecue for 2 to 3 minutes. Remove from the barbecue and cut into wedges. Serve immediately.

Yield: 4 main-dish servings

Curried Cauliflower
and Carrots en Papillote

INGREDIENTS

300g cauliflower florets

260g diced carrots

4 large cloves garlic,
    peeled and sliced

55g unsalted butter, melted

2 tbsps (28ml) cooking sherry

1 tsp curry powder

$^1/_4$ tsp salt

175g uncooked orzo or other
    soup pasta

4g finely chopped
    fresh coriander

4 lime wedges

This is a fancy and flavourful way to serve cauliflower and carrots. The accent of the coriander and lime finishes the dish.

Place a baking stone on the barbecue and preheat the barbecue to medium-high before you are ready to cook the packets. (See 'How to Make and Assemble *en Papillote* Packets' on page 104 for instructions on how to use this cooking technique.)

Distribute the cauliflower, carrots, and garlic evenly among four 45 x 50cm pieces of greaseproof paper or heavy-duty foil, positioning them near the centre of each crease. Set aside.

Melt the butter in a small pan and add the sherry, curry powder, and salt. Drizzle an equal amount over each mound of vegetables.

Close the greaseproof paper or heavy-duty foil packets. When ready to cook, place the packets in a single layer on the baking stone and bake for about 15 minutes.

Meanwhile, heat water in a medium-size saucepan on the hob over high heat for the orzo (or other soup pasta). When the water is boiling, add the orzo. Reduce the heat to medium-high and cook for about 15 minutes. Drain the orzo into a colander.

Transfer the packets to warmed serving plates. Have each diner pinch and tear the paper to release the aromatic steam. The contents may then be lifted out onto the plates and the papers removed from the table. Serve the cooked orzo. Have diners sprinkle the coriander and squeeze the lime juice over the dish as desired.

Yield: 4 main-dish servings

Potatoes, Mushrooms, and Shallots en Papillote

Serve this elegantly presented but comforting dish with cheese and crusty bread for a lovely meal.

INGREDIENTS

700g red potatoes, diced

455g button mushrooms, sliced

4 shallots, peeled and sliced

55g butter, melted

60ml cooking sherry

2 tsps horseradish

2 tsps dried oregano

1/2 tsp salt

Several grinds black pepper,
  to taste

1kg fresh spinach

1 tbsp (14ml)
  white vinegar

6 large eggs

Place a baking stone on the barbecue and preheat the barbecue to medium-high before you are ready to cook the packets. (See 'How to Make and Assemble *en Papillote* Packets' on page 105 for instructions on how to use this cooking technique.)

Distribute the potatoes, mushrooms, and shallots evenly among six 45 x 50cm pieces of greaseproof paper or heavy-duty foil, positioning them near the centre of each crease.

Mix the butter, sherry, horseradish, oregano, salt, and black pepper together in a small bowl or measuring cup. Pour equal amounts of the butter mixture over the individual vegetable packets.

Close the kitchen parchment or heavy-duty foil packets. When ready to cook, place the packets in a single layer on the baking stone and bake for 15 to 20 minutes.

Meanwhile, remove the stems from the spinach and place the leaves in a colander. Rinse well to remove any dirt. Place the wet spinach in a large stock pot on the hob over medium-high heat, cover, and steam for 5 minutes. Transfer the spinach to a colander to drain. Return the spinach to the stock pot, cover, and keep warm.

Place a shallow pan on the hob and fill with water. Cover and bring to a boil. Add the vinegar and reduce the heat to a strong simmer. Stir the water in a circular motion and carefully add each egg. (Add each egg directly from the cracked shell or break an egg into a saucer and slip it gently from the saucer into the water.) As the eggs cook, use a large spoon to dip some water from around the sides of the eggs and pour it over them to cook the tops. When a film forms over the yolks and the whites are firm, the eggs are cooked. (This takes about 5 minutes.)

Transfer the packets to warmed serving plates. Place equal amounts of spinach on each plate and top with a poached egg. Have each diner pinch and tear the paper to release the aromatic steam. The contents may then be lifted out onto the plates and the papers removed from the table.

Yield: 6 main-dish servings

Asparagus, Shiitake Mushrooms, and Tofu en Papillote

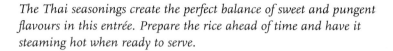

INGREDIENTS

- 400g extra-firm tofu
- 455g asparagus
- 225g fresh shiitake mushrooms
- 75ml unsweetened coconut milk
- 3 tbsps (3g) finely chopped coriander
- I tsp freshly squeezed lemon juice
- 2 cloves garlic, finely chopped
- I tsp soy sauce
- I tsp grated fresh ginger
- Pinch cayenne pepper
- 390 to 585g cooked brown basmati rice

The Thai seasonings create the perfect balance of sweet and pungent flavours in this entrée. Prepare the rice ahead of time and have it steaming hot when ready to serve.

Place a baking stone on the barbecue and preheat the barbecue to medium-high before you are ready to cook the packets. (See 'How to Make and Assemble *en Papillote* Packets' on page 105 for instructions on how to use this cooking technique.)

Rinse the tofu and cut it in half through the middle, then into 12 strips. Wash the asparagus and snap off and discard the tough ends. Cut the asparagus at a slant into 3cm pieces. Remove and discard the stem ends from the mushrooms and slice the caps. Set aside.

In a small bowl, stir together the coconut milk, coriander, lemon juice, garlic, soy sauce, ginger, and cayenne pepper.

Distribute the asparagus spears lengthwise among four 45 x 50cm pieces of greaseproof paper or heavy-duty foil, positioning them near the centre of each crease. Top with equal amounts of the mushrooms. Place an equal number of tofu strips on top of the asparagus. Pour the sauce evenly over the tofu.

Close the greaseproof paper or heavy-duty foil packets. When ready to cook, place the packets in a single layer on the baking stone and bake for about 15 minutes.

Transfer the packets to warmed serving plates. Have each diner pinch and tear the paper to release the aromatic steam. The contents may then be lifted out onto the plates and the papers removed from the table. Serve the cooked basmati rice.

Yield: 4 main-dish servings

Summer Squashes
en Papillote with Tex-Mex Seasonings

INGREDIENTS

1 tsp cumin seed

1 tsp chilli powder

1/2 tsp granulated garlic

1/8 tsp salt

Several grinds black pepper,
   to taste

455g summer squashes, cubed or
   whole if small

1 red bell pepper, thinly sliced

1 small onion, diced

6 tsps finely chopped
   fresh coriander

4 tsps dry white wine

2 tsps olive oil

2 tbsps (20g) raw, unsalted
   pumpkin seeds

390g cooked brown rice

345g cooked black beans

You may use any type of summer squash for this dish, but a colourful variety looks best. If you can find bite-size baby squashes, you can cook them whole for a stunning effect. Cook the rice and black beans before you are ready to serve the packets and serve them steaming hot. Serve Pear and Avocado Salsa (page 39) for a perfect accompaniment.

Place a baking stone on the barbecue and preheat the barbecue to medium-high before you are ready to cook the packets. (See 'How to Make and Assemble *en Papillote* Packets' on page 105 for instructions on how to use this cooking technique.)

Use a mortar and pestle or spice grinder to crush the cumin seeds.

In a small bowl, stir together the cumin seed, chilli powder, garlic, salt, and black pepper. Set aside.

Distribute the squash, bell pepper, and onion evenly among four 45 x 50cm pieces of greaseproof paper or heavy-duty foil, positioning them near the centre of each crease. Sprinkle equal amounts of the spice mixture and coriander over the vegetables. Drizzle 1 tsp of the wine and 1/2 tsp of the olive oil over each packet.

Close the greaseproof paper or heavy-duty foil packets. When ready to cook, place the packets in a single layer on the baking stone and bake for about 15 minutes.

Meanwhile, place the pumpkin seeds in a single layer in a heavy, dry frying pan on the hob over medium heat. Shake or stir the seeds frequently. When they begin to pop, keep the seeds moving. (You want them to pop but not get too brown.) Remove the pumpkin seeds from the pan, let them cool a bit, and mince them. Set the pumpkin seeds aside in a small serving dish.

Transfer the packets to warmed serving plates. Have each diner pinch and tear the paper to release the aromatic steam. The contents may then be lifted out onto the plates and the papers removed from the table. Serve the cooked brown rice, black beans, and pumpkin seeds.

Yield: 4 main-dish servings

Broccoli and Mushrooms
en Papillote with Paprika, Feta, and Dill Seed

INGREDIENTS

1 tsp paprika

1/2 tsp crushed dill seed

Pinch salt

Several grinds black pepper,
   to taste

570g broccoli

115g button mushrooms

1/2 red onion, thinly sliced

60ml dark beer

85g crumbled feta cheese

4 lemon wedges

390 to 585g cooked brown
   basmati rice

This delectable dish features the distinctive flavours of Eastern Europe. The ingredients are available year-round, so enjoy this dish any time you want to fire up the barbecue. Have the rice cooked and steaming hot when you are ready to serve.

Place a baking stone on the barbecue and preheat the barbecue to medium-high before you are ready to cook the packets. See 'How to Make and Assemble *en Papillote* Packets' on page 105 for instructions on how to use this cooking technique.)

In a small bowl, combine the paprika, dill seed, salt, and black pepper. Cut off and discard the tough stem ends of the broccoli and peel the remaining stalks if they are particularly thick-skinned. Cut the broccoli lengthwise into even-size spears. Bush or wipe loose dirt particles from the mushrooms and quarter them.

Distribute the broccoli spears evenly among four 45 x 50cm pieces of greaseproof paper or heavy-duty foil, positioning them near the centre of each crease. Add one-quarter of the mushrooms and onion to each packet, arranging loosely on top of the broccoli. Sprinkle equal amounts of the paprika mixture over the vegetables and pour equal amounts of the beer over each portion. Top with equal amounts of feta cheese. Close the greaseproof paper or heavy-duty foil packets.

When ready to cook, place the packets in a single layer on the baking stone and bake for about 15 minutes. Transfer the packets to warmed serving plates. Have each diner pinch and tear the paper to release the aromatic steam. The contents may then be lifted out onto the plates and the papers removed from the table. Serve with the lemon and pass round the cooked basmati rice.

Yield: 4 main-dish servings

Summer Squash Stuffed
with Sweet Pepper Couscous en Papillote

INGREDIENTS

175g uncooked couscous

235ml white wine

60ml freshly squeezed lemon juice

3 tsps granulated garlic

2 small yellow butternut squashes

4 small courgette

2 scallop squashes

25g finely diced
   red bell pepper

25g finely diced
   yellow bell pepper

25g finely diced green bell pepper

I jalapeño chilli, seeded and
   finely chopped

I large egg, beaten

I tbsp (14ml) extra-virgin olive oil

45g manchego cheese, grated

This en papillote dish is best prepared wrapped in one large foil packet. All of the flavours steam together as they cook – the resulting dish is delicious. Manchego cheese is a semi-hard sheep-milk cheese from Spain.

Place the couscous in a bowl and add 100ml of the wine and the lemon juice and garlic. Stir to combine and set aside for 5 to 10 minutes.

Preheat the barbecue to medium-high. Cut the crookneck squashes, courgette, and scallop squashes in half lengthwise and remove the seeds from the butternut squash. Use a spoon or melon baller to scoop out the flesh centres, being careful to leave at least a 1cm-thick shell. Place 175g of the pulp in a bowl and add the bell peppers and jalapeño chilli. Stir to combine. Add the couscous along with the egg and olive oil. Stir to incorporate. Stuff each squash cavity with the couscous filling and place on a large sheet of foil. Top with the manchego cheese.

Crimp the edges of the packet and pour the remaining wine into the packet, then fold over the top and sides to seal. Place the packet on the barbecue and cook for 15 to 18 minutes. Remove the packet from the barbecue and place on a large platter or on individual serving plates and serve immediately.

Yield: 6 main-dish servings

CHAPTER 7

Pasta, Grain, and Polenta Dishes

In this chapter, it is not necessarily the pasta, grain, or polenta that is barbecued, but the components that go into the dish are, yielding a delicious meal. Several recipes feature barbecued polenta – a fabulous way to serve this humble cornmeal – but most use the pasta or grain as the base to showcase the barbecued items. It is critical, however, to master the art of preparing perfectly cooked pasta, rice, and polenta.

Every excellent pasta dish begins with excellent pasta. Italian households typically use dried pasta made of semolina flour and water, and this variety is preferred for most recipes in this chapter. That said, when preparing an Asian-themed dish, use soba noodles, made from buckwheat flour.

Cooking pasta is simple – bring a large pot of water to a boil on the hob and add the pasta. The caveat is placing the proper amount of water in the pot and determining the cooking time. Plenty of water, 6 to 8 litres per pound of pasta, will prevent the pasta from sticking to the pot. Bring the water to a strong, rolling boil, then add the pasta and stir it vigorously a few times while it is cooking.

Pasta should be cooked *al dente*. The Italian phrase literally means 'to the tooth', suggesting that the tooth should meet a little resistance when biting into the pasta. Recommended cooking times vary and are usually listed on the pack. Set your timer for a couple of minutes less than the recommended time, and when the timer goes off, remove a noodle from the pot. If it is undercooked, it will stick to your teeth when you bite into it. Continue to cook, testing again every minute or so, until the pasta is tender but not mushy. This is the sought-after al dente stage. As you master cooking pasta, you will be able to look at it and tell when it is done! Drain the al dente pasta immediately in a large, footed colander. Shake the colander to remove excess water, but do not rinse the pasta.

Rice is best prepared in a pot that has a tight-fitting lid and is the appropriate size for the amount of rice that you are cooking. Add the rice to rapidly boiling water, then cover and cook it over very low heat. Whole grain rice, such as brown rice, takes the longest to cook, so put it on at least 45 minutes before you plan to serve the meal. Basmati rice is a fragrant variety from India and a favourite of mine. You will find brown and white basmati, both of which should be rinsed right before cooking. This removes some of the starch and yields fluffy rice. Brown basmati cooks in about 35 minutes, while the white basmati takes only about 20 minutes.

Risotto dishes use a unique, oval, short-grained rice – usually Fino Arborio – that releases its starch gradually during the cooking process to create a creamy texture. Do not rinse Arborio rice before cooking because you do not want to wash away any of the surface starches. Cook risotto in an open pot, adding small amounts of liquid as it cooks. To prevent sticking or scorching, stir risotto almost constantly as it absorbs each addition of liquid. If risotto sticks despite stirring, reduce the heat slightly. If the recommended amount of liquid is absorbed before the rice is tender, add more hot stock or water, half a cup at a time, until the rice is tender and the consistency for the risotto is creamy, not sticky.

The last grain showcased in this chapter is polenta. Basically cornmeal mush elevated to gastronomic heights by innovative seasonings and toppings, polenta is served either creamy and soft, or firm. Soft polenta is always served hot, while the firm style is shaped in a loaf and barbecued.

Polenta is best cooked in a heavy-bottomed saucepan on the hob. Essential tools include a whisk for adding the polenta to the boiling water and a long-handled wooden spoon for stirring as the polenta thickens. To avoid lumps in the finished dish, add the polenta to the hot water gradually over the course of a minute or two, pouring in a slow, steady stream. Whisk continuously while you are adding it to the water. For polenta that is to be served creamy and soft, prepare it to come off the stove right before serving. For firm, barbecued polenta such as Barbecued Polenta with Tomato Coulis (page 147), prepare the polenta in advance and allow it to set up in a loaf pan for several hours before slicing and barbecuing it.

The barbecued ingredients of each of these recipes play the starring role in the dish. Some dishes are seasonal, like the Pasta with BBQ Asparagus and Onions (page 135), Risotto with Barbecued Corn and Red Peppers (page 142), and Vermicelli with Barbecued Tomato Sauce (page 126). Other recipes call for ingredients that are more seasonless. Enjoy Barbecued Portobello Mushrooms with Couscous and Gruyère Cheese (page 134) or Pistachio-Encrusted Tofu with Basmati Rice (page 141) any time of the year.

Pasta with BBQ Asparagus
and Onions

INGREDIENTS

75ml extra-virgin olive oil

3 tbsps (45ml) freshly squeezed
lemon juice

3 tsps finely chopped
fresh tarragon

3 tsps finely chopped fresh flat-
leaf parsley

I tbsp (I5g) Dijon mustard

$1/2$ tsp salt

Several grinds fresh black pepper,
to taste

3 red torpedo-shaped onions

2 tbsps (28ml) olive oil

Ikg fresh asparagus

Pinch salt

455g rotini pasta

Grated parmesan cheese
(optional)

I like this pasta dish in the spring, when you can purchase fresh onions and asparagus at the farmers' market. Choose the thickest asparagus stalks you can to produce the best succulent results. I like a rotini or fusilli pasta for this dish. This dish is best made ahead of time and served at room temperature.

Prepare the dressing by whisking together the extra-virgin olive oil, lemon juice, tarragon, parsley, mustard, $1/2$ tsp salt, and black pepper in a small bowl. Set aside.

Preheat the barbecue to medium. Trim and discard the green tops and root ends from the onions and peel them. Slice them lengthwise, brush with some of the olive oil, and set aside.

Wash the asparagus carefully to remove any traces of soil. Snap off the tough ends. Place the asparagus in a plastic bag and drizzle with the remaining olive oil. Twist the bag to seal, allowing some of the air to remain in the bag. Toss gently to coat the asparagus evenly.

Place the onions on the barbecue. Grill the onions for 15 to 18 minutes until they are soft, but not falling apart, turning twice. Remove the asparagus from the bag, place on a barbecue grate, and transfer to the barbecue. Barbecue the asparagus for 8 to 10 minutes, sprinkling with the pinch of salt and turning frequently so the stalks cook but do not burn. Barbecue just until al dente; they will be slightly charred. Remove the onions and asparagus from the barbecue and set aside.

Meanwhile, bring several litres of water to a boil in a large stock pot on the hob and cook the pasta until al dente. Transfer the pasta to a colander and rinse with cold water to stop the cooking. Drain thoroughly. Transfer the pasta to a large bowl.

Place the onions on a cutting board and slice. Cut the asparagus into 3cm pieces. Add the onions and asparagus to the pasta and toss to combine. Drizzle with the dressing and toss again. Set aside for about an hour or so to allow the flavours to develop. Serve at room temperature. Pass grated Parmesan cheese, if desired.

Yield: I0 side-dish servings

Vermicelli with Barbecued Tomato Sauce

INGREDIENTS

1.25kgs pear tomatoes

2 medium onions

1 large bulb garlic

2 tbsps (28ml) olive oil

6 tsps fresh oregano

455g vermicelli

Grated Parmesan cheese
  (optional)

You might not think of barbecuing tomatoes, but this recipe will prove that they are delicious prepared this way. Serve with a chickpea salad and Bruschetta (page 70) for an unforgettable meal.

Preheat the barbecue to medium. Remove and discard the stem ends of the tomatoes, but leave them whole. Peel the onions and cut them in half. Break the garlic into individual cloves and peel them. Set the garlic aside.

Put the tomatoes directly on the barbecue. Rub the onions with 1 tbsp of the olive oil and place them on the barbecue cut side down. Barbecue the onions for about 30 minutes, turning occasionally, until tender. Turn the tomatoes frequently as they cook. (The skins will char and some of their juice will drip off.) Coat the garlic with the remaining tbsp olive oil. Place the garlic in a barbecue basket and place on the barbecue for about 10 to 15 minutes, turning several times, until slightly charred and tender.

Remove the tomatoes, onions, and garlic from the barbecue and place in a food processor. Puree until slightly smooth. Add the oregano and puree to combine.

Meanwhile, bring several litres of water to a boil in a large stock pot on the hob and cook the pasta until al dente. Drain the pasta and place it in a large serving bowl. Top with the sauce, toss gently, and serve immediately. Pass grated Parmesan cheese, if desired.

Yield: 6 main-dish servings

Fusilli Pasta in Caper Cream Sauce
with Barbecued Aubergine and Red Pepper Strips

INGREDIENTS

1 medium aubergine

3 tsps coarse salt

2 large red bell peppers

2 tbsps (28ml) olive oil

340g fusilli pasta

75ml dry white wine

3 tbsps (45g) butter

3 tbsps (25g) unbleached flour

410ml whole milk

3 tbsps (8g) finely chopped
   fresh basil

3 tbsps (25g) finely
   chopped capers

Grated Parmesan cheese
   (optional)

The tartness of the capers in this recipe is the perfect compliment to the rich, creamy sauce.

Cut off the stem and bottom end of the aubergine and discard. Slice the aubergine crosswise into slices about 1.5cm thick. Remove the aubergine's bitter juices by sprinkling both sides of the slices with the salt and place them on a rack for about 30 minutes. (The salt will cause the aubergine to 'sweat' and release the bitter juices.) Briefly rinse the slices and blot dry with kitchen paper.

Meanwhile, preheat the barbecue to medium-high. Place the bell peppers directly on the barbecue for 10 to 15 minutes, turning frequently. (The pepper skins will be charred black.) Transfer the peppers to a plastic or paper bag, close the bag, and set aside for about 15 minutes. When the peppers are cool enough to handle, peel off the skins and discard the seeds, stems, and white membranes. Coarsely chop the peppers and set aside in a warm spot.

Brush each side of the aubergine slices with the olive oil and place the slices on the barbecue. Barbecue for 5 to 8 minutes until lightly browned, turn, and continue to barbecue for another 5 to 8 minutes. (The aubergine should be tender-crisp, not mushy.) Remove the aubergine from the barbecue, cut into cubes, and set aside in a warm spot.

While the vegetables are barbecuing, fill a large stock pot with water for the pasta and place on the hob over high heat. Bring to a boil and add the pasta. Cook for 6 to 8 minutes, until al dente. Drain and place in a warm bowl.

While the pasta is cooking, heat the milk in a microwave or on the hob to scalding, but don't allow it to boil.

Melt the butter over medium heat in a heavy-bottomed frying pan. Sift in the flour and cook for about a minute, whisking constantly. Add the hot milk, a little at a time, whisking constantly until it is incorporated. Continue to cook over medium-low heat for about 8 minutes. Add the wine, basil, and capers to the sauce. Stir in the aubergine and bell peppers. Heat through for a minute or two. Pour the sauce over the pasta. Gently toss to combine. Pass grated Parmesan cheese, if desired.

Yield: 4 main-dish servings

Marinated BBQ Aubergine
with Bowtie Pasta

INGREDIENTS

4 Japanese aubergines

2 tbsps (28ml) olive oil

425g cooked red beans

455g green beans

60ml extra-virgin olive oil

2 tbsps (28ml)
   red wine vinegar

1 tsp crushed garlic

10g chopped fresh basil

15g chopped fresh
   flat-leaf parsley

6 tsps snipped fresh chives

$^1/_4$ tsp salt

455g bowtie pasta

55g Parmesan cheese,
   shaved into thin strips

Aubergine soaks up flavour, so it is the perfect vegetable to carry the flavours of the fresh herbs in this outstanding pasta entrée. Choose the narrow, elongated aubergine variety – known as Japanese or Asian aubergine – for this dish. Use a kidney or another red bean variety to add a spark of colour.

Preheat the barbecue to medium. Remove and discard the stem ends from the aubergines and slice lengthwise. Brush the cut sides of the aubergines with the olive oil and place on the barbecue skin sides down. Barbecue for 2 to 3 minutes, turn, and barbecue 2 to 3 minutes more. (The aubergine will develop barbecue marks and become slightly soft.) Remove the aubergines from the barbecue to a cutting board. Slice lengthwise and coarsely chop. Place the aubergine in a large bowl along with the red beans.

Trim the ends from the green beans and cut them into 3cm pieces. Place the green beans on a steamer rack in a saucepan with a tight-fitting lid and cook on the hob over medium-high heat for 8 to 10 minutes, just until fork-tender. Drain the green beans and plunge them into ice water to stop the cooking and set their bright green colour. Add the green beans to the bowl with the aubergine and red beans.

In a separate bowl, whisk together the extra-virgin olive oil, red wine vinegar, garlic, basil, parsley, chives, and salt. Pour the mixture over the aubergine and beans and marinate at room temperature for about an hour, tossing occasionally.

Bring several litres of water to a boil in a large stock pot on the hob and cook the pasta until al dente. Transfer the pasta to a colander to drain. Place the pasta in a large shallow serving bowl and spoon the aubergine and beans over the top. Drizzle with all of the marinade left in the bowl. Gently toss to combine. Top with the Parmesan cheese and serve immediately.

Yield: 8 main-dish servings

Fettuccine with
Barbecued Sweet-Potato Puree

INGREDIENTS

3 medium red-skinned
  sweet potatoes

2 medium red bell peppers

475ml low-fat milk

2 tbsps (28g) unsalted butter

2 tbsps (15g) unbleached flour

$1/4$ tsp salt

Several grinds black pepper,
  to taste

$1/8$ tsp freshly
  grated nutmeg

$1/4$ tsp ground cinnamon

455g fettuccine

60ml dry sherry

Grated Parmesan cheese
  (optional)

This recipe was inspired by a dish that I enjoyed at a restaurant in New York City near Central Park. The thought of sweet potatoes and pasta had never occurred to me. This dish, with its red bell pepper garnish, is stunning on the plate, and it's simply delicious.

Preheat the barbecue to medium-high. Wash the sweet potatoes and pierce in several places with a fork. Place the sweet potatoes on the barbecue and barbecue for about 45 minutes, until they are soft, turning occasionally. Place the bell peppers on the barbecue. Cook for about 30 minutes, turning frequently to evenly char the skin. (The skins will blacken as they cook.) Remove the peppers, place them in a plastic or paper bag, and allow them to cool. When the peppers are cool enough to handle, peel off the blackened skins. Remove and discard the stems, seeds, and white membranes. Slice the peppers into 1.5cm strips and set aside.

Remove the sweet potatoes from the barbecue and place them on a cutting board. Allow them to cool slightly, peel off the charred skins, and dice. Place them in a food processor with a quarter of the milk and 60ml water. Puree until smooth and set aside.

Meanwhile, put several litres of water on to boil in a stock pot on the hob over high heat. On the hob, melt the butter in a large frying pan over medium-low heat. Whisk in the flour, allow to cook a moment, and then gradually whisk in the remaining milk. Add the salt, black pepper, nutmeg, and cinnamon. Cook the sauce for about 10 minutes, stirring frequently. Simultaneously, cook the fettuccine in the boiling water until al dente, about 8 to 10 minutes.

Add the sweet potato puree and sherry to the white sauce, whisk to combine, and heat through. Drain the fettuccine and place in a large warmed serving bowl. Toss with the sweet potato sauce and arrange the barbecued bell pepper strips over the top. Serve immediately. Pass grated Parmesan cheese, if desired.

Yield: 6 main-dish servings

Pasta with BBQ Artichokes
and Fresh Shiitake Mushrooms

INGREDIENTS

3 medium artichokes

85g fresh shiitake mushrooms

3 tbsps (45ml) olive oil

I tsp crushed garlic

455g fusilli pasta

2 tbsps (28g) butter

2 tbsps (15g) unbleached flour

2 tbsps (28ml) dry sherry

355ml low-fat milk

85g coarsely grated
    Asiago cheese

3 tsps finely chopped
    fresh tarragon

3 tsps finely chopped
    flat-leaf parsley

$1/4$ tsps salt

Several grinds black pepper,
    to taste

Barbecued artichokes develop a subtle smoky flavour that pairs well with this pasta dish, complementing the strong flavour of the shiitake mushrooms.

Snap off the small, tough outer leaves at the base of the artichokes and trim off the pointy ends at the top. Trim and discard any sharp points from the mid-range leaves. Leave most of the stems, just trimming off the bottom ends. Put a steaming rack in a large saucepan and place the artichokes on the rack, leaves pointed down. Add several inches of water to the pan and cover tightly. Bring the water to a boil on the hob, reduce the heat to medium, and steam for about 25 minutes, until al dente. Remove the artichokes from the pan to a cutting board. Cool for several minutes. Using a sharp knife, cut the artichokes in half lengthwise. Spoon out and discard the chokes – the fuzzy fibres – leaving the leaves attached to the bottom.

Remove the stem ends from the mushrooms and place on a cutting board, gill sides up.

Place 2 tbsps of the olive oil in a small bowl and whisk in the garlic. Distribute equal amounts of the oil mixture into the gills of each mushroom, reserving some to brush on the bottom side of each mushroom.

Meanwhile, preheat the barbecue to medium-high. Rub the cut sides of the artichokes with the remaining 1 tbsp olive oil and place the artichokes cut sides down on the barbecue. Grill for about 2 minutes until barbecue marks appear, turn, and grill for 2 more minutes. Place the mushrooms on the barbecue, bottom sides down. Grill for 2 minutes, turn, and grill for 2 more minutes. Remove the artichokes and mushrooms from the barbecue and place on a platter. Set aside and keep warm.

Bring several litres of water to a boil in a large stock pot on the hob for the pasta. Add the pasta and cook for 6 to 8 minutes, until al dente.

While the pasta is cooking, melt the butter in a frying pan on the hob over medium-low heat, then stir in the flour and sherry. Cook for about 1 minute, stirring constantly, being careful not to scorch the flour. Add the milk, a bit at a time, whisking to incorporate as the sauce thickens. Stir in the Asiago cheese and allow it to melt. Add the tarragon, parsley, salt, and black pepper.

Drain the pasta and place it in a large shallow serving bowl. Pour the sauce over the top and toss to coat. Arrange the artichoke halves on top of the pasta, cut sides up. Cut the mushrooms into strips and distribute over the top of the pasta. Serve immediately.

Yield: 6 main-dish servings

Barbecued Portobello Mushrooms
with Couscous and Gruyère Cheese

INGREDIENTS

175g uncooked couscous

2 jalapeño chillies,
    seeded and diced

1 tbsp (14g) unsalted butter

$1/4$ tsp mild chilli powder

$1/4$ tsp granulated garlic

4 medium portobello mushrooms

60ml plus 1 tsp olive oil

2 tbsps (28ml) sweet chilli sauce

60ml dry white wine

120g loosely packed grated
    Gruyère cheese

6 tsps finely chopped
    fresh coriander

This recipe combines ingredients from many different cuisines, making it a real fusion dish. Most of the ingredients can be found readily at any supermarket, but you may need to go to an Asian food shop for the sweet chilli sauce.

Place 355ml water in a saucepan on the hob and bring to the boil. Add the couscous, jalapeño chillies, butter, chilli powder, and garlic. Stir to combine, cover, and then remove from the heat. Set aside for at least 5 minutes, undisturbed.

Meanwhile, preheat the barbecue to high with a smoker box in place. Remove the stem ends from the mushrooms and wipe the caps with damp kitchen paper to remove any dirt. Place the mushrooms on a work surface, gill sides up. Evenly distribute the 60ml olive oil and sweet chilli sauce over the gills of the mushrooms. Allow the mushrooms to absorb the olive oil mixture for about 15 minutes. Pour equal amounts of the wine into the gill side of each mushroom. Rub the bottom of the mushrooms with the reserved 1 tsp olive oil and transfer them to the barbecue, gill sides up. Barbecue for 3 to 4 minutes, turn, and continue to barbecue for an additional 3 to 4 minutes. Remove the mushrooms from the barbecue and place on a cutting board. Cut into thick slices.

To serve, place equal amounts of the couscous on 4 warm plates. Top with equal amounts of mushroom slices. Sprinkle with the Gruyère cheese and coriander, then serve immediately.

Yield: 4 main-dish servings

Pasta with Barbecued Fennel

and Asparagus

INGREDIENTS

I bulb fennel, feathery tops
   removed

2 tbsps (28ml) olive oil

455g asparagus

340g egg noodles

475ml whole milk

3 tbsps (45g) butter

I shallot, finely finely chopped

3 tbsps (25g) unbleached flour

13g sun-dried tomatoes,
   reconstituted and
   finely chopped

1/4 tsp salt

Several grinds black pepper,
   to taste

1/4 tsp freshly grated nutmeg

The creamy sun-dried tomato sauce lightly coats the pasta and enhances the barbecued vegetables in this dish. Nutmeg is the secret ingredient in this recipe, serve some at the table if you wish.

Preheat the barbecue to medium-high. Cut off and discard the top and bottom of the fennel and cut the bulb in half. Cut out and discard the inner core. Cut the halves into quarters and thinly slice. Place the fennel in a bag and add 1 tbsp of the olive oil. Twist the bag to seal, allowing some air to remain in the bag. Toss gently to coat the fennel evenly. Place a barbecue grate on the barbecue and add the fennel from the bag. Barbecue for 8 to 10 minutes, turning the pieces occasionally. Remove the fennel from the barbecue and set aside in a warm spot.

Snap off and discard the tough ends from the asparagus and cut them into 3cm pieces. Place the asparagus in the bag and add the remaining 1 tbsp olive oil. Twist the bag to seal, allowing some air to remain in the bag. Toss gently to coat the asparagus evenly. Add the asparagus from the bag to the barbecue grate and cook, turning occasionally, for 8 to 10 minutes until tender-crisp. Remove the asparagus from the barbecue and set aside in a warm spot.

Meanwhile, fill a large stock pot with water for the noodles and place on the hob over high heat. Bring to a boil and add the noodles. Cook for 6 to 8 minutes until al dente. Drain and place in a warm bowl.

While the pasta is cooking, heat the milk in a microwave or on the hob to scalding, but don't allow it to boil.

Melt the butter over medium heat in a heavy-bottomed frying pan on the hob. Add the shallot and sauté for a minute or two. Sift in the flour and cook about a minute, whisking constantly. Add the hot milk a little at a time, whisking constantly until it is incorporated. Continue to cook over medium-low heat for about 10 minutes until thickened. Add the sun-dried tomatoes to the sauce. Stir in the salt, black pepper, and nutmeg. Pour over the drained noodles and toss to combine. Add the barbecued fennel and asparagus, toss again, and serve immediately.

Yield: 6 main-dish servings

Lasagna with Barbecued Corn,
Kalamata Olives, and Fresh Tomato Sauce

INGREDIENTS

1kg tomatoes

2 tbsps (28ml) olive oil

3 tsps crushed garlic

2 tbsps (40g) honey

2 tbsps (28ml) red wine

6 tsps finely chopped fresh
oregano

2 ears corn, in husks

455g ricotta cheese

100g Barbecued Kalamata
Olives (page 61)

370g fresh lasagna noodles

28g fresh Parmesan cheese,
thinly sliced

The corn, tomatoes, and cheese in this recipe meld together to create a light, summer-style lasagna. If you have a burner on your barbecue, you can prepare the entire dish outside. If you cannot locate fresh noodles and do not want to prepare them at home, use dried lasagna noodles and cook as instructed on the pack before layering in this dish.

Cut the tomatoes in half crosswise and gently squeeze out the seed pockets. Coarsely chop the tomatoes and set aside.

Place the olive oil in a frying pan over medium heat on the hob and add the garlic. Sauté for a minute, and then add the tomatoes. Increase the heat to medium-high and sauté for about 15 minutes, stirring occasionally. Add the honey, red wine, and oregano and continue to cook for about 10 more minutes.

Meanwhile, place the corn in a plastic bag and fill the bag with water to soak the husks for about 15 minutes. Preheat the barbecue to high. Remove the corn from the bag of water and place on the barbecue. Turn every few minutes to evenly blacken all sides of the husks. Barbecue for 18 to 22 minutes. (The kernels will steam in the husks.) Remove the corn from the barbecue. Allow the corn to cool, then peel off the husks and remove the silk. Cut the corn from the cob and set aside in a bowl. Mix in the ricotta cheese. Chop the Barbecued Kalamata Olives and add them to the corn mixture, stirring to combine. Reduce the barbecue heat to medium-low.

Place $^1/_3$ of the tomato sauce evenly over the bottom of a 25 x 35-cm baking dish. Place a layer of noodles to cover, then half of the corn-ricotta mixture. Add another layer of noodles, $^1/_3$ more sauce, and the remaining corn-ricotta mixture. Top with the remaining noodles and tomato sauce. Cover with foil and place on the barbecue. Cook for 45 minutes, until the sauce is bubbling, then remove the foil and top with the Parmesan cheese. Continue to cook for about 10 minutes. Remove from the barbecue and cool for about 15 minutes before slicing into 6 equal portions.

Yield: 6 main-dish servings

BBQ Bok Choy
with Green Curry Rice

Curry paste is a wonderful, but spicy, ingredient. You will find prepared green, red, and yellow curry pastes in any Asian market. Use a small amount to start with, you can always add more if you like it spicy. Serve this with chutney and lemon slices.

INGREDIENTS

455g baby bok choy

2 tbsps (28ml) pure sesame oil

180g uncooked basmati rice

400ml light coconut milk

2 tsps green curry paste

235ml low-fat milk

Yield: 4 main-dish servings

Preheat the barbecue to medium-high. Rinse the bok choy and shake to remove some of the water. Cut any large heads in half lengthwise. Place the bok choy in a plastic bag and drizzle with the sesame oil. Twist the bag to seal, allowing some air to remain in the bag. Toss gently to coat the bok choy evenly. Remove the bok choy from the bag and place on the barbecue. Cook for 3 to 5 minutes, turning frequently, until the leaves are limp and slightly charred. Remove the bok choy from the barbecue, coarsely chop, and set aside.

Meanwhile, heat 475ml water to a boil in a medium saucepan on the hob. Add the basmati rice, reduce the heat to low, and simmer for about 20 minutes. Remove the saucepan from the heat, fluff the rice with a fork, and set aside.

Place the coconut milk in a medium saucepan and whisk in the green curry paste. Heat over medium heat until just simmering and add the bok choy and milk. Cook for about 5 minutes.

Spoon equal amounts of rice into 4 individual serving bowls. Top each with equal amounts of the bok choy-curry mix. Serve at once.

Basmati Rice with
Barbecued Summer Squashes

INGREDIENTS

6 small assorted summer
   squash

1 tbsp (14ml) olive oil

180g uncooked basmati rice

3 tbsps (45ml) extra-virgin
   olive oil

2 tbsps (28ml) red
   wine vinegar

1 tsp Dijon mustard

$1/4$ tsp salt

Several grinds black pepper,
   to taste

6 tsps chopped fresh oregano

225g cherry tomatoes, halved

4 spring onions, thinly sliced

8 fresh squash blossoms
   (optional)

Use an assortment of small summer squashes to add colour to this fragrant rice dish. If you grow squash, harvest eight squash blossoms to use as garnishes. You may also find fresh blossoms at your local farmers' market, or perhaps a generous gardening neighbour would be willing to share.

Preheat the barbecue to medium-high. Remove and discard the stem ends from the squashes and cut them in half lengthwise. Place the squashes in a plastic bag and add the olive oil. Twist the bag to seal, allowing some of the air to remain in the bag. Toss gently to coat the squashes evenly. Remove the squashes from the bag and place them on the barbecue. Grill for 8 to 10 minutes until tender-crisp, turning twice. Remove the squashes from the barbecue, coarsely chop, and set aside.

Meanwhile, place 475ml water in a saucepan on the hob and bring to a boil. Place the basmati rice in a fine mesh strainer and rinse, drain thoroughly, then stir it into the boiling water. Cover, reduce the heat to very low, and simmer for about 15 to 20 minutes until all of the water is absorbed. Turn off the heat and allow the saucepan to stand for at least 5 minutes before serving.

While the rice is cooking, whisk together the extra-virgin olive oil, red wine vinegar, mustard, salt, and black pepper until emulsified. Add the oregano and whisk again to combine. Set aside.

Place the rice in a shallow serving bowl. Add the barbecued summer squashes, tomatoes, and spring onions. Drizzle with the olive oil mixture and gently toss to combine. Garnish with the squash blossoms, if desired, and serve immediately.

Yield: 4 main-dish servings

Saffron Rice with
Barbecued Fennel, Asparagus, and Leeks

INGREDIENTS

2 medium leeks

24 spears asparagus

1 bulb fennel

2 tbsps (28ml) olive oil

2 tbsps (28g) unsalted butter

260g uncooked long-grain
white rice

1/4 tsp saffron threads

1 tbsp (14ml) extra-virgin
olive oil

1 tbsp (14ml) balsamic vinegar

Grated Parmesan cheese
(optional)

*Saffron adds a delicate flavour and a bright yellow colour to the rice.
The barbecued vegetables are aromatic and have a tender-crisp texture.*

Trim off and discard the green tops and root ends from the leeks.
Cut the leeks in half lengthwise and thoroughly rinse each half to
remove any sand. Set aside.

Snap off and discard the tough ends from the asparagus spears.
Set aside.

Remove and discard the feathery top portion of the fennel.
Slice the bulb in half lengthwise, then cut each half into 4 slices.
Remove and discard the tough centre cores. Set aside.

Preheat the barbecue to high with a smoker box in place. Put
the fennel and leeks in a plastic bag and add 1 tbsp of the olive oil.
Twist the bag to seal, allowing some air to remain in the bag. Toss
gently to coat the fennel and leeks evenly. Place a barbecue basket
on the barbecue grate and add the fennel from the bag. Barbecue
for 10 to 12 minutes until tender-crisp, turning several times.
Meanwhile, add the leeks to the barbecue basket and barbecue for 8
to 10 minutes until tender-crisp, turning several times. Remove the
fennel and leeks from the barbecue, place on a cutting board, tent
with foil, and keep warm. Put the asparagus in the bag and drizzle
with the remaining 1 tbsp olive oil. Twist the bag to seal, allowing
some air to remain in the bag. Toss gently to coat the asparagus
evenly. Remove the asparagus from the bag, place on the barbecue,
and cover the barbecue. Grill for 8 to 10 minutes, turning
frequently, until the asparagus is al dente and slightly charred.

Meanwhile, place 700ml water in a saucepan on the hob and
bring to a boil. Add the butter and then stir in the rice. Crumble
the saffron threads over the rice and stir to incorporate. Cover the
saucepan, reduce the heat to very low, and cook for about 15
minutes, until the water is absorbed and the rice is tender.
Remove from the heat.

Chop the barbecued fennel, asparagus, and leeks, and drizzle
with the extra-virgin olive oil and balsamic vinegar. Mound equal
amounts of rice on 4 warm serving plates and top with the barbecued vegetables. Serve immediately with grated Parmesan cheese,
if desired.

Yield: 4 main-dish servings

Barbecued Courgettes
over Mint-Pesto Risotto

INGREDIENTS

3 medium courgettes

3 tbsps (45ml) olive oil

830 ml Vegetable Stock
(page 23)

2 tbsps (28ml) dry white wine

2 shallots, finely chopped

200g uncooked Arborio rice

175g Mint Pesto (page 23)

Grated Romano cheese
(optional)

The Mint Pesto (page 23) gives this dish a bright flavour and vibrant colour. Use homemade Vegetable Stock (page 29) or a commercially prepared version.

Preheat the barbecue to medium-high. Remove and discard the stem ends from the courgettes and cut them lengthwise into $^3/_4$-cm slices. Place the courgettes in a plastic bag and drizzle with 1 tbsp of the olive oil. Twist the bag to seal, allowing some of the air to remain in the bag. Toss gently to coat the courgettes evenly. Place the courgettes on the barbecue and cook for about 10 minutes until tender-crisp, turning twice. Remove the courgettes from the barbecue, slice into matchsticks, and set aside.

Meanwhile, heat the Vegetable Stock in a saucepan on the hob until steaming and keep it handy near the stove.

Place the remaining 2 tbsps olive oil and the wine in a heavy-bottomed saucepan on the hob over medium heat and add the shallots. Cook for about a minute, then add the rice. Stir to coat the rice. Add the stock, a little at a time, stirring almost constantly and waiting until the liquid is absorbed before adding the next bit. When the last little bit of stock has been absorbed and the rice is tender, remove from the heat and stir in the Mint Pesto.

Spoon the rice into bowls and top with equal amounts of the barbecued courgettes strips. Serve immediately with grated Romano cheese, if desired.

Yield: 4 main-dish servings

Pistachio-Encrusted Tofu
with Basmati Rice

INGREDIENTS

800g extra-firm tofu

180g uncooked brown
   basmati rice

115g Double Gloucester, sliced

65g finely chopped
   pistachio nuts

2 tbsps (28ml) olive oil

2 tbsps (28g) unsalted butter

2 tbsps (15g) unbleached flour

250g Vegetable Stock
   (page 23)

200g Boysenberry Sauce
   (page 33)

My friend Lizz Blaise and I came up with the concept for this elegant presentation of tofu that tastes as good as it looks. The drizzle of berry sauce on the plate and over the barbecued tofu adds the final touch.

Cut the slabs of tofu through the middle to create 4 pieces. Place each piece on sheet of kitchen paper and cover with another sheet. Place a heavy frying pan on top to press the excess water from the tofu. After 15 minutes, place the slabs between fresh towels and repeat the process.

Meanwhile, bring 475ml water to a boil in a medium-sized saucepan on the hob. Put the basmati rice in a fine mesh strainer and rinse. Add the rice to the boiling water, return to a boil, reduce the heat to very low, cover, and simmer for 40 to 45 minutes, until all of the water is absorbed. Remove the saucepan from the heat and set aside until needed.

Preheat the barbecue to medium. Place the tofu on a work surface and place one-quarter of the Double Gloucester on two of the slabs. Sprinkle with half of the nuts, then top with the remaining cheese. Cover with the remaining two slabs of tofu, as you would when making a sandwich, to create 2 cheese-filled tofu steaks. Brush the top and bottom of each steak with the olive oil. Press equal amounts of the remaining nuts into the outside of each steak, top and bottom. Place the tofu in a barbecue basket and clamp to encase the tofu steaks. Set aside.

Melt the butter in a frying pan over low heat on the hob and whisk in the flour to form a thick paste. Increase the heat to medium and gradually add the Vegetable Stock, whisking to incorporate. Whisk in the Boysenberry Sauce and continue to cook until the sauce thickens, about 3 to 4 minutes. Cover and set aside.

Place the tofu steaks, in the barbecue basket, on the barbecue and barbecue for 4 to 6 minutes, turning several times. (The cheese will melt and the tofu will develop barbecue marks.) Drizzle 6 warm serving plates with some of the sauce. Cut the tofu steaks in thirds, creating 6 individual portions. Place one on each plate and drizzle with the remaining sauce. Serve the rice.

Yield: 6 main-dish servings

Risotto with Barbecued Corn
and Red Peppers

INGREDIENTS

4 ears yellow corn, not husked

2 medium red bell peppers

830ml Vegetable Stock
(page 29)

2 tbsp (28g) unsalted butter

2 cloves garlic, finely chopped

$1/4$ tsp ground cumin

I tsp mild chilli flakes

60ml dry sherry

200g uncooked Arborio rice

10g chopped fresh basil

Several grinds black pepper,
to taste

25g finely grated
Parmesan cheese

Fresh corn is a favourite summertime vegetable, so serve it in a variety of ways when it is in season. Use homemade Vegetable Stock (page 23) or a ready-made version to flavour the risotto in this colourful dish.

Place the corn in a plastic bag and fill the bag with water to soak the husks for about 15 minutes. Meanwhile, heat the barbecue to high. Cut each bell pepper lengthwise from the stem to create 8 slices. Discard the stems, seeds, and white membranes. Place the peppers on the barbecue and barbecue for about 2 minutes per side, until they soften and char slightly. Remove the peppers from the barbecue. When the peppers are cool enough to handle, without peeling, coarsely chop and set aside.

Remove the corn from the bag and place directly on the barbecue. Turn every few minutes to evenly blacken all sides of the husks. Barbecue for 18 to 22 minutes. (The kernels will steam in the husks.) Remove the corn from the barbecue. When the corn is cool enough to handle, peel off the husks and silk. (Use tea towel to hold the corn as you husk it if it is too hot to touch.) Return the corn to the barbecue to slightly char, turning and cooking for about 5 minutes. Working with one ear at a time, hold one end of the cob upright and place the other end on a cutting board. Take a sharp knife and cut the corn kernels from the cob, being careful not to cut through the cob itself. Place the kernels in a bowl and set aside.

Meanwhile, heat the Vegetable Stock in a saucepan on the hob until steaming and keep it handy near the stove.

Melt the butter in a heavy-bottomed saucepan on the hob over medium heat and add the garlic, cumin, and chilli flakes. Cook for about a minute, then add the sherry and Arborio rice. Stir to coat the rice. Add the stock, a little at a time, stirring almost constantly, and waiting until the liquid is absorbed before adding the next amount. Add the corn and bell pepper with the last of the stock. When the all the stock has been absorbed and the rice is tender, add the basil, black pepper, and Parmesan cheese. Stir to incorporate and serve immediately.

Yield: 4 main-dish servings

Portobello Mushrooms
in Mustard Marinade over Green Risotto

INGREDIENTS

45g lightly packed fresh basil

30g lightly packed fresh spinach

120ml plus $^1/_4$ tsp olive oil

3 tsps crushed garlic

65g Dijon mustard

3 tbsp (45ml)
   extra-virgin olive oil

2 tbsps (28ml) freshly squeezed
   lemon juice

$^1/_8$ tsp salt

Several grinds black pepper,
   to taste

4 small portobello mushrooms

1 tbsp (14g) butter

2 tbsp (28ml) cooking sherry

200g uncooked Arborio rice

830ml Vegetable Stock (page 23)

Fresh basil and spinach give the risotto in this recipe its green colour. The mustard-infused portobello mushrooms finish the dish to perfection.

Place the basil, spinach, 120ml olive oil, and 1 tsp of the garlic in a food processor and puree. Set aside.

Combine the mustard, extra-virgin olive oil, lemon juice, salt, and black pepper in a bowl and whisk together.

Cut off the stem ends of the mushrooms and reserve for another use. With the gill sides up, distribute equal amounts of the mustard sauce in each mushroom. Marinate for about 10 minutes.

Meanwhile, melt the butter in a heavy-bottomed saucepan on the hob and add the sherry. Add the Arborio rice and stir to coat. Add the Vegetable Stock, a little at a time, stirring almost constantly and waiting until the liquid is absorbed before adding the next small amount. Add the basil puree with the last bit of stock.

While the rice is cooking, preheat the barbecue to medium-high. Rub the $^1/_4$ tsp olive oil on the cap sides of the mushrooms and place them on the barbecue, cap sides down (gill sides up). Barbecue for 8 to 10 minutes, until fork-tender. Remove the mushrooms from the barbecue, slice, and briefly set aside in a warm spot.

Spoon the risotto into 4 warm shallow bowls. Arrange the mushroom slices on top and serve immediately.

Yield: 4 main-dish servings

Barbecued Polenta
with Tomato Coulis

INGREDIENTS

1/2 tsp dried thyme

I tsp salt

125g uncooked polenta

35g finely grated Parmesan
  cheese

2 tbsps (28g) unsalted butter

I tbsp (14ml) olive oil

235ml Tomato Coulis (page 24)

Grated Parmesan cheese
  (optional)

You can serve this barbecued polenta in many ways. When tomatoes are in season, the fresh Tomato Coulis (page 24) is the perfect topping. During the winter, you may want to serve it with a mushroom sauce. The polenta does require some time to set up before barbecuing, so prepare it in advance. Serve this with a barbecued or steamed seasonal vegetable and a light red wine.

Bring 475ml water to a boil in a heavy-bottomed saucepan on the hob over medium-high heat. Crush the thyme between the palms of your hands, then add it to the water along with the salt. Gradually pour in the polenta in a slow, steady stream, whisking constantly. Reduce the heat to medium-low and gently simmer for about 20 minutes, stirring almost constantly with a wooden spoon. (The polenta will thicken as it cooks.) Add the Parmesan cheese and butter during the last few minutes of cooking time. When the polenta is thick enough to pull away from the sides of the pan, pour the polenta into a small loaf pan and set aside to firm up for about 30 minutes. (You may set it aside for several hours, depending on your time frame.)

Preheat the barbecue to medium-high. Slice the polenta into 4 thick slices, or 8 thinner ones, depending on the size of the pan that you used as the mould. Brush the polenta slices with the olive oil and place on the barbecue. Barbecue for 5 to 6 minutes, turn, and continue to grill for 4 to 5 minutes. (The slices will develop barbecue marks.)

Meanwhile, heat the Tomato Coulis in a small saucepan.

Place the barbecued polenta slices on individual warmed serving plates and top with the Tomato Coulis. Serve with additional grated Parmesan cheese, if desired.

Yield: 4 main-dish servings

Polenta with Broccoli Rabe
and Portobello Mushrooms

INGREDIENTS

1 large red bell pepper

125g uncooked polenta

60g grated cheddar cheese

25g finely grated
   Parmesan cheese

2 large portobello mushrooms

120ml olive oil

120ml Soy and Balsamic Fusion
   Marinade (page 26)

4 cloves garlic, finely chopped

1 1/2 tsps lemon juice

700g broccoli rabe
   (also known as chinese
   flowering cabbage. You could
   substitute swiss chard or
   mustard greens)

This delicious meal comes together in several stages. You can make the sauce in advance, then the polenta. Keep the polenta warm while you barbecue the mushrooms and broccoli rabe. The presentation is beautiful.

Preheat the barbecue to medium-high. Place the bell pepper directly on the barbecue and cook for 10 to 15 minutes, turning frequently. Barbecue until the skin is charred black. Transfer the pepper to a plastic or paper bag, close the bag, and set aside for about 15 minutes. When the pepper is cool enough to handle, remove and discard the stem end, seeds, and white membrane. Dice the pepper and set aside.

Heat 1 litre water to a boil in a medium sauce pan on the hob. Gradually pour in the polenta in a slow, steady stream, whisking constantly. Reduce the heat to medium-low and simmer for about 20 minutes, stirring almost constantly with a wooden spoon. When the polenta is thick enough to begin to pull away from the sides of the pan, add the cheddar cheese, Parmesan cheese, and bell pepper. Stir to combine. Cover and keep warm until serving. Stir in a tbsp or two of hot water just before serving if the polenta appears to be too thick.

Meanwhile, cut off the stem ends of the mushrooms and set aside for another use. Lightly rub a small amount of olive oil on the cap side of the mushrooms. With the gill sides up, distribute 2 tbsps of the Soy and Balsamic Fusion Marinade into each mushroom. Place the mushrooms gill sides up on the barbecue and grill for 8 to 10 minutes, until fork-tender. Remove from the barbecue and briefly set aside. Cut into slices before serving.

While the mushrooms are cooking, whisk together the olive oil, garlic, and lemon juice. Place the broccoli rabe on a plate and drizzle with the oil mixture. Place the broccoli rabe on the barbecue and grill for 3 to 5 minutes, until wilted. Turn frequently. Remove from the barbecue, then trim off and discard the stem ends. Fan the broccoli rabe onto 4 warm plates. Top with equal amounts of polenta and mushroom slices. Serve immediately.

Yield: 4 main-dish servings

BBQ Onions and Courgettes
with Gorgonzola Polenta

INGREDIENTS

2 small onions

2 tbsps (28ml) olive oil

3 medium courgettes

I tbsp (14ml)
    balsamic vinegar

2 tsps crushed garlic

$^1/_4$ tsp salt

125g uncooked polenta

2 tbsps (28g) unsalted butter

3 tbsps (10g) fresh sage
    leaves, finely chopped

55g crumbled Gorgonzola
    cheese

Fresh sage leaves (optional)

This soft, creamy polenta is the perfect base for the balsamic-infused onions and courgettes. This dish has several steps, but it comes together easily – and it's delicious!

Preheat the barbecue to medium-high. Trim off the ends of the onions and peel them, then cut in half across the middle. Rub 1 tbsp of the olive oil over the cut ends. Place the onions, cut sides down, directly on the barbecue. Barbecue for 25 to 30 minutes, turning every 8 to 10 minutes. (The onions are done when they are soft and slightly charred.)

Meanwhile, remove and discard the stem ends from the courgettes and cut lengthwise into $^3/_4$-cm slices. Place the courgettes in a plastic bag and add the remaining 1 tbsp olive oil, the balsamic vinegar, 1 tsp garlic, and the salt. Twist the bag to seal, allowing some of the air to remain in the bag. Toss gently to coat the courgettes evenly. Remove the courgettes from the bag, place on the barbecue, and cook for about 10 minutes, until tender-crisp, turning twice.

While the vegetables are cooking, bring 1 litre water to a boil in a saucepan on the hob over medium-high heat for the polenta. Add the remaining 1 tsp garlic, then whisk in the polenta, adding it in a slow, steady stream. Reduce the heat to low and gently simmer for about 20 minutes, stirring almost constantly with a wooden spoon. (As it cooks, the polenta will thicken.)

Melt the butter in a small pan over medium-low and add the sage. Cook for about 3 to 4 minutes, remove from the heat, and set aside. When the polenta is done, strain the sage butter into it, discarding the sage. Stir in the Gorgonzola cheese and mix to combine.

Spoon equal amounts of polenta onto 4 warm serving plates. Place half of an onion on each plate and arrange equal amounts of courgettes over each portion of polenta. Garnish with additional fresh sage, if you wish. Serve immediately.

Yield: 4 main-dish servings

Barbecued Corn
and Cheddar Cheese Polenta

This recipe has several steps, but the results are worth the effort. Serve with Salsa Fresca (page 45) or your favourite commercially prepared salsa.

INGREDIENTS

2 ears corn, not husked

2 tbsps (28g) butter

2 jalapeño chillies, seeded and
    finely chopped

190g uncooked polenta

225g grated cheddar cheese

1 tsp granulated garlic

1/2 tsp salt

1 tsp mild chilli powder

Salsa Fresca (page 45)
    or prepared salsa

Place the corn in a plastic bag and fill the bag with water to soak the husks for about 15 minutes. Meanwhile, preheat the barbecue to high. Remove the corn from the bag of water and place on the barbecue. Turn every few minutes to evenly blacken all sides of the husks. Barbecue for 18 to 22 minutes. (The kernels will steam in the husks.) Remove the corn from the barbecue. Allow the corn to cool, then peel off the husks and remove the silk. Cut the kernels from the cob and set aside in a bowl.

Meanwhile, melt the butter over low heat in a large saucepan on the hob and add the jalapeño chillies. Sauté for a couple of minutes, then 1.5 litres hot water. Increase the heat to high and bring to a boil. Gradually pour in the polenta in a slow, steady stream, whisking constantly. Reduce the heat to medium-low and gently simmer for about 20 minutes, stirring almost constantly with a wooden spoon. (The polenta will thicken as it cooks.) Add the cheddar cheese and corn during the last few minutes of cooking time, along with the garlic, salt, and chilli powder. When the polenta is thick enough to pull away from the sides of the pan, pour into 8 individual 12-cm ramekins and allow to firm up for about 30 minutes. (You may set the ramekins aside for several hours, depending on your time frame.)

Run a thin knife blade around the rim of each ramekin and turn the polenta out onto a cutting board. Place the polenta directly on the barbecue and barbecue for about 3 minutes on each side, turning with a wide spatula. Remove the polenta from the barbecue and serve immediately, passing your favourite salsa.

Yield: 8 main-dish servings

BBQ Aubergine Parmesan
with Soft Polenta

The aubergine in this dish is barbecued, not fried, providing the perfect base for the creamy, soft polenta, tomato and cheese.

INGREDIENTS

1 medium aubergine

3 tsps coarse salt

570g) plum tomatoes

3 tbsps (45ml) olive oil

2 cloves garlic, finely chopped

$1/4$ tsp salt

2 tbsps (28ml) red wine

3 tsps finely chopped
　fresh oregano

55g Parmesan cheese, shaved
　into thin strips

125g uncooked polenta

100g finely grated
　Parmesan cheese

1 tbsp (14g) unsalted butter

Fresh oregano sprigs (optional)

Cut off the stem and bottom ends of the aubergine and slice crosswise into slices about $1^{1}/_{2}$-cm thick. To rid the aubergine of its bitter juices, sprinkle both sides of the slices with the coarse salt and place them on a rack for about 30 minutes. (The salt will cause the aubergine to 'sweat' and release the bitter juices.) Briefly rinse the aubergine and blot dry with kitchen paper.

Meanwhile, cut the tomatoes in half crosswise and gently squeeze out the seed pockets. Chop the tomatoes coarsely and set side.

Heat 1 tbsp of the olive oil in a sauté pan over medium heat on the hob and add the garlic. Stir and sauté briefly, then add the tomatoes and salt. Cook, uncovered, over a medium-high heat for about 10 minutes, until the tomatoes are soft and have released their liquid. Stir in the red wine and oregano and continue to cook for about 5 minutes, until a chunky sauce develops. Set aside.

Preheat the barbecue to high. Brush each side of the aubergine slices with the remaining 2 tbsps olive oil and place on the barbecue. Barbecue the aubergine for 5 to 8 minutes until browned, turn, and continue to barbecue for another 5 to 8 minutes. Remove the aubergine from the barbecue to a large plate. Top with equal amounts of the tomato sauce and distribute the shaved Parmesan cheese over the sauce. Set the aubergine aside in a warm spot.

Heat 1 litre water to a boil in a medium saucepan on the hob. Gradually pour in the polenta in a slow, steady stream, whisking constantly. Reduce the heat to medium-low and simmer for about 20 minutes, stirring almost constantly with a wooden spoon. When the polenta is thick enough to begin to pull away from the sides of the pan, add the grated Parmesan cheese and butter. Stir to combine. Cover and keep warm until needed. Stir in a tbsp or two of hot water just before serving if the polenta appears to be too thick.

Carefully place the aubergine slices back on the barbecue and heat for about 2 minutes to warm them. To serve, place equal amounts of polenta on 6 warm plates. Flatten slightly, then top with aubergine slices. Garnish with oregano sprigs, if desired.

Yield: 6 main-dish servings

CHAPTER 8

Skewered Entrées

Skewered entrées are easy to prepare and elegant to serve. Wooden skewers are best for tofu dishes, because the succulent ingredients may fall apart when skewered with sharp metal skewers. Soak wooden skewers in water for at least 10 minutes before threading with the recipe ingredients to prevent the skewers from scorching on the barbecue. If they begin to burn while the ingredients are cooking, place a strip of foil on the barbecue under the ends of the skewers to prevent the heat from singing them. If you use metal skewers, the cooking time will be slightly less, as the metal will transmit heat to the food from within.

Food cooks quickly on skewers, but some of the recipes require time for the ingredients to marinate. Prepare the marinades in advance and allow the ingredients to soak up the delicious flavours. Tofu Sates (page 167) and Curry-Marinated Tofu Skewers with Jalapeño and Lime (page 159) are sure to become favourites. Reserve the marinade to pour over the skewers as they barbecue or pour over the entrée when served.

Dipping sauces are the perfect accompaniment to serve with skewered entrées because the cubes of food are just the right size for dipping. I've made suggestions in some of the recipes, but read through 'Salsas, Chutneys, and Dipping Sauces,' beginning on page 34, for additional ideas. Serve the Dilled Yogurt and Sour Cream Sauce (page 51) with Tofu in Garlic-Soy Marinade (page 166), and try the Spicy Tahini Sauce (page 50) with Tempeh, Mushroom, and Cherry Tomato Skewers (page 163).

Have the rest of the meal prepared and just about ready to serve when you put the skewers on the barbecue. Spray or brush some oil on the barbecue rack, then place the skewers crosswise on the barbecue. Most skewered entrées cook in just 15 to 20 minutes, but they need to be turned several times while they are cooking. Some recipes call for two skewers to be threaded side by side so the ingredients will not twist around on the skewers. Serve the skewers on a large warm platter or on individual serving plates. Allow diners to remove the barbecued ingredients from the skewers at the table.

Tempeh, Pineapple, and Jalapeño Skewers

INGREDIENTS

120ml unsweetened coconut milk

2 tbsps (28ml)
  unseasoned rice vinegar

1 tbsp (14ml) toasted sesame oil

1 tbsp (14ml) soy sauce

225g soy tempeh, cut into 24 cubes

6 jalapeño chillies, cubed

155g cubed pineapple

225g soba noodles

Serve these skewers with Peanut Sauce (page 46) or Mango and Papaya Salsa with Jalapeños (page 37) to bring all of the flavours together. Soba noodles, made with buckwheat flour, are delicious with this dish.

Soak 8 wooden skewers in water. Place the coconut milk, rice vinegar, sesame oil, and soy sauce in a medium bowl and whisk together. Pour into a loaf pan and add the tempeh. Gently toss to combine. Set aside to marinate for about 30 minutes.

Preheat the barbecue to medium-high. Start with a cube of jalapeño chilli and alternately thread the tempeh and pineapple on each skewer. End with a cube of jalapeño pepper. Repeat with the remaining ingredients to fill all 8 skewers. Place the skewers on the barbecue and barbecue for 12 minutes, turning several times. Spoon some of the reserved marinade over the skewers while they barbecue. Reserve the remaining marinade to spoon over the soba noodles when they are served.

Meanwhile, in a large stock pot, heat several litres of water to a boil over high heat on the hob. Add the soba noodles and stir gently, bring back to a boil, and cook for about 5 minutes, until the soba noodles are tender but not mushy. Drain well and distribute between 4 warm serving plates.

Top each with two tempeh skewers and serve immediately. Drizzle with any remaining marinade.

Yield: 4 main-dish servings

Courgette, Onion, and Red Bell Pepper Skewers

INGREDIENTS

455g pearl onions

2 large red bell peppers

455g courgettes,
   cut into 3cm rounds

60ml olive oil

I tbsp (14ml)
   balsamic vinegar

2 tsps crushed garlic

1/4 tsp salt

Dilled Yogurt and Sour Cream
   Sauce (page 51)

Crusty fresh bread or Bruschetta
   (page 67)

Various cheeses

Summer vegetable gardens provide so much fresh produce – such a treat for us to barbecue! When the garden is overflowing, invite a few friends over and prepare this simple dish. Use yellow and green courgettes and red and yellow peppers for a particularly pleasing presentation. Serve with Dilled Yogurt and Sour Cream Sauce (page 51). Serve with crusty fresh bread or Bruschetta (page 67) and a selection of cheeses.

Soak 12 wooden skewers in water. Put several litres of water in a large saucepan and heat to a boil on the hob. Place the onions in a blanching basket, place it in the boiling water, bring back to a boil and cook for about a minute. Plunge the onions into cold water and slip off the skins. Leave the onions whole and set aside.

Preheat the barbecue to medium-high with a smoker box in place. Stem and seed the bell peppers and cut into 3cm cubes. Place the onions, bell peppers, and courgettes in a plastic bag. Drizzle with the olive oil and balsamic vinegar and add the garlic. Twist the bag to seal, allowing some of the air to remain in the bag. Toss gently to coat the vegetables evenly.

Start with a cube of bell pepper and alternately thread the onions and courgettes on each skewer. Repeat with the remaining skewers to fill all 12 skewers. Place on the barbecue and barbecue for 12 to 15 minutes, turning several times.

Place the skewers on a large warm plate Put individual plates on the table for your guests. Serve the Dilled Yogurt and Sour Cream Sauce along with the bread or Bruschetta and cheeses of your choice.

Yield: 6 main-dish servings

Red Potato and
Mushroom Skewers

The Basil Pesto (page 27) pasta forms a flavourful base for the barbecued vegetables, and the presentation is beautiful.

INGREDIENTS

570g small red potatoes

60ml olive oil

340g small button mushrooms

I tsp soy sauce

I tsp crushed garlic

175g Basil Pesto (page 23)

60g sour cream

225g capellini pasta

Grated Parmesan cheese
  (optional)

Soak 6 wooden skewers in water. Preheat the barbecue to medium-high. Scrub the potatoes but do not peel them. Place the potatoes in the microwave oven and cook them for about 5 minutes, until slightly soft but not completely cooked. (They will finish cooking on the barbecue.) When the potatoes are cool enough to handle, cut them into uniform chunks. Set the potatoes aside in a medium bowl and drizzle with 2 tbsps of the olive oil.

Meanwhile, brush the dirt from the mushrooms and trim the stem ends to be flush with the bottom of each mushroom. Reserve the stems for another use.

In a medium bowl, whisk together the remaining 2 tbsps olive oil and the soy sauce and garlic. Place the mushrooms in the bowl and toss to combine. Set aside.

Place the Basil Pesto in a small bowl and whisk in the sour cream. Set aside.

Bring several litres of water to a boil in a large stock pot on the hob for the pasta. Skewer the potatoes and mushrooms, alternating them on the skewers, and set aside. Add the pasta to the pot of boiling water and cook for 6 to 8 minutes, until al dente. While the pasta is cooking, place the skewers on the barbecue and grill for 6 to 8 minutes, turning several times.

Whisk 60ml of the pasta cooking water into the pesto mixture. Drain the pasta in a colander and place it in a shallow bowl. Add the pesto mixture and toss to combine. Place equal amounts of pasta on 6 warm serving plates. Top with skewers of potatoes and mushrooms and serve immediately. Serve with grated Parmesan cheese, if desired.

Yield: 6 main-dish servings

Curry-Marinated Tofu Skewers
with Jalapeño and Lime

INGREDIENTS

120ml unsweetened
   coconut milk

2 tbsps (28ml) freshly
   squeezed lime juice

1 tbsp (14ml) toasted
   sesame oil

2 tsps curry powder

$1/4$ tsp salt

800g extra-firm tofu

4 limes

4 jalapeño chillies, sliced

180g uncooked basmati rice

Dilled Yogurt and Sour
   Cream Sauce (page 51)
   (optional)

Tofu will accept almost any flavour, and here curry is the star. Serve this Middle Eastern-inspired dish with Dilled Yogurt and Sour Cream Sauce (page 51).

Soak 8 wooden skewers in water. In a small bowl, whisk together the coconut milk, lime juice, sesame oil, curry powder, and salt. Set aside.

Cut the slabs of tofu through the middles to create 4 pieces. Place each piece on a sheet of kitchen paper, cover with another sheet, and place a heavy frying pan on top to remove excess moisture. After 15 minutes, place the slabs between fresh paper and repeat the process. Cut each slab into 6 pieces to form cubes.

Place about half of the curry marinade in a shallow baking dish and add the tofu in a single layer. Pour the remainder of the marinade over the top. Marinate for about an hour, gently turning the pieces after about 30 minutes.

Preheat the barbecue to medium-high. Cut each lime into 8 wedges. Start with a lime wedge and alternately thread the tofu, jalapeño chillies, and lime wedges on each skewer, ending with a lime wedge, to create 8 threaded skewers. Reserve any residual marinade. Place the skewers on the barbecue and barbecue for about 20 minutes, turning several times.

Meanwhile, bring 475ml water to a boil in a medium-sized saucepan on the hob. Put the basmati in a fine mesh strainer and rinse. Add the rice to the boiling water, return to a boil, reduce the heat to very low, cover, and simmer for 15 to 20 minutes, until all of the water is absorbed.

Mound equal amounts of rice on 4 warm serving plates and top each serving with 2 skewers. Drizzle with any remaining curry marinade. Serve with the Dilled Yogurt and Sour Cream Sauce, if desired.

Yield: 4 main-dish servings

Skewered Tofu and Tomatoes

INGREDIENTS

800g extra-firm tofu

Honey-Ginger Marinade (page 27)

225g cherry tomatoes

140g uncooked bulgur

This is a fast, simple dish that is perfect with a fresh green salad. I always use extra-firm tofu, since it can be cut into cubes and skewered without falling apart. Choose a mixture of different colours of cherry tomatoes (red, yellow, orange) for a stunning presentation.

Soak 16 wooden skewers in water. Cut the slabs of tofu through the middle to create 4 pieces. Place each piece on a sheet of kitchen paper, cover with another sheet, and place a heavy frying pan on top to remove excess moisture. After 15 minutes, place the slabs between fresh paper to repeat the process. Cut each slab into 6 pieces to form cubes.

Place about half of the Honey-Ginger Marinade in a shallow baking dish and add the tofu in a single layer. Pour the remainder of the marinade over the top. Marinate for about an hour, gently turning the pieces after about 30 minutes.

Preheat the barbecue to high. Using 2 skewers per serving, place them about 1$^{1}/_{2}$-cm apart, threading each piece onto both skewers at once. Start with a tomato and alternately thread the tofu and tomatoes on each skewer to create 8 double-threaded skewers. Reserve any residual marinade. Place the skewers on the barbecue and barbecue for about 20 minutes, turning several times.

Meanwhile, bring 475ml water to a boil in a medium-sized saucepan on the hob. Add the bulgur, return to a boil, reduce the heat to very low, cover, and simmer for 15 minutes. Turn off the heat without disturbing the lid and set aside for 5 minutes.

Mound equal amounts of bulgur on 4 warm serving plates and top each serving with 2 skewers. Drizzle with the reserved marinade.

Yield: 4 main-dish servings

Spicy Peanut Tofu Skewers
with a Trio of Bell Peppers

INGREDIENTS

130g smooth peanut butter

90ml dry sake

60ml freshly squeezed
    lemon juice

2 tbsps (28ml) peanut oil

3 tsps chilli flakes

800g extra-firm tofu

455g bell peppers

180g uncooked jasmine rice

Use green, red, and yellow bell peppers for this tasty and colourful entrée. The marinade is spicy, so if you prefer a milder dish, use half the amount of chilli flakes. You can serve this with a dipping sauce, if desired.

Soak 8 bamboo skewers in water. In a small bowl, whisk together the peanut butter, sake, lemon juice, peanut oil, and chilli flakes. Set aside.

Cut the slabs of tofu through the middle to create 4 pieces. Place each piece on a sheet of kitchen paper, cover with another, and place a heavy frying pan on top to remove excess moisture. After 15 minutes, place the slabs between fresh paper to repeat the process. Cut each slab into 6 pieces to form cubes.

Place about half of the peanut marinade in a shallow baking dish and add the tofu in a single layer. Pour the remainder of the marinade over the top. Marinate for about an hour, gently turning the pieces after about 30 minutes.

Remove and discard the stem ends of the bell peppers and cut them in half. Cut out and discard the membrane and seeds. Slice the halves in half and then into about 3-cm cubes.

Preheat the barbecue to medium-high. Skewer the bell peppers and tofu, starting with a bell-pepper cube, and alternately thread the tofu and bell-pepper cubes, ending with a bell-pepper cube, to create 8 threaded skewers. Reserve any residual marinade. Place the skewers on the barbecue and barbecue for about 20 minutes, turning several times.

Meanwhile, bring 475ml water to a boil in a medium-sized saucepan on the hob. Put the jasmine rice in a fine mesh strainer and rinse. Add the rice to the boiling water, return to a boil, reduce the heat to very low, cover, and simmer for 15 to 20 minutes until all of the water is absorbed. Mound equal amounts of rice on 4 warm serving plates and top each serving with 2 skewers. Drizzle with any reserved marinade.

Yield: 4 main-dish servings

Tempeh, Mushroom, and Cherry Tomato Skewers

INGREDIENTS

60ml dry sake

3 tbsps (45ml) soy sauce

2 tbsps (28ml) sesame oil

3 tsps grated fresh ginger

2 tsps dry wasabi

2 tsps rice vinegar

455g soy tempeh

270g uncooked brown
   basmati rice

225g cremini mushrooms

455g cherry tomatoes

Spicy Tahini Sauce (page 51)

Creamy Ponzu Sauce (page 51)

The flavours in this easy dish blend to create a delicious and satisfying entrée. The ginger in the marinade adds a delightful fragrance to the kitchen as the tempeh marinates. Choose cherry tomatoes in variety of different colours for a particularly pleasing presentation. Serve with Spicy Tahini Sauce (page 50) or Creamy Ponzu Sauce (page 51).

Soak 12 wooden skewers in water. Place the sake, soy sauce, sesame oil, and ginger in a small bowl and whisk together.

In a separate small bowl, whisk together the wasabi and rice vinegar to form a paste. Add to the sake mixture, whisk to combine the two, and set aside.

Cut the tempeh into 40 small squares. Put the squares in a shallow dish and pour the sake mixture over them. Marinate for about 30 minutes, tossing occasionally.

Meanwhile, place 700ml water in a saucepan over high heat on the hob. Bring to a boil. Rinse the rice, stir it into the water, return to a boil, cover, and reduce the heat to very low. Simmer for about 45 minutes, then turn off the heat and allow to sit undisturbed for at least 5 minutes.

Preheat the barbecue to medium. Remove the stems from the mushrooms and reserve for another use. Thickly slice the mushrooms. Start with a cherry tomato and alternately thread the tempeh, mushrooms, and cherry tomatoes on the skewers, ending with a cherry tomato. Repeat with the remaining ingredients to fill all 12 skewers. Reserve the marinade. Place the skewers on the barbecue and barbecue for 10 minutes, turning several times. Pour the reserved marinade over the skewers as they barbecue.

Place equal amounts of rice on 6 warm serving plates. Top each serving with 2 skewers. Serve the Spicy Tahini Sauce or Creamy Ponzu Sauce dipping sauces as desired.

Yield: 6 main-dish servings

Tofu Sates

INGREDIENTS

800g extra-firm tofu

3 stalks lemon grass

2 cloves garlic, finely
    chopped

I Thai chilli or jalapeño chilli,
    seeded and finely chopped

I tsp ground coriander

$1/2$ tsp ground turmeric

2 tbsps (28ml) freshly
    squeezed lime juice

175ml unsweetened
    coconut milk

3 tbsps (45ml) soy sauce

2 tbsps (40g) honey

185g uncooked long-grain
    brown rice

Peanut Sauce (page 53) or
    Creamy Ponzu Sauce
    (page 57) (optional)

Sates are small kebabs on a stick. I make this tofu version by marinating the tofu in a rich sauce that is a combination of coconut milk, spices, and minced Thai chilli or jalapeño chillies. Prepare your own sauce as shown below or purchase a commercially prepared version from the supermarket or Asian market. I like to serve this as an entrée, but it is also a delightful appetizer. Serve it with Peanut Sauce (page 53) or Creamy Ponzu Sauce (page 57) if you wish.

Soak 8 wooden skewers in water. Cut the slabs of tofu through the middle to create 4 pieces. Place each piece on a sheet of kitchen paper, cover with another sheet, and place a heavy frying pan on top to remove excess moisture. After 15 minutes, place the slabs between fresh sheets to repeat the process. Cut each slab into 6 pieces to form cubes.

Meanwhile, trim off and discard the root ends and top green ends from the lemon grass stalks. Discard the tough outer layers and mince the tender inner cores.

Place the lemon grass, garlic, Thai chilli or jalapeño chilli, coriander, and turmeric in a mortar and use the pestle to pound into a fragrant paste. Add the lime juice and pound to combine. Transfer to a ceramic or glass bowl and stir in the coconut milk, soy sauce, and honey.

Place half of the sauce in a shallow baking dish and add the tofu. Pour the remaining sauce over the top. Marinate for about an hour, gently turning the cubes after about 30 minutes.

Meanwhile, place 525ml water in a saucepan on the hob and bring to a boil. Add the rice, cover the saucepan, and reduce the heat to very low. Cook for 40 to 45 minutes, until all of the water is absorbed.

Preheat the barbecue to high. Thread the tofu on the skewers, creating 8 threaded skewers. Reserve any residual marinade. Place the skewered tofu on the barbecue and cook for about 20 minutes, turning several times. Pour some of the reserved sauce over the tofu skewers as they barbecue, reserving the remainder of the sauce to pass at the table.

Remove the skewers from the barbecue. Spoon equal amounts of rice on 4 warm serving plates and top each with 2 tofu skewers. Drizzle with reserved marinade and serve with Peanut Sauce or Creamy Ponzu Sauce, if desired.

Yield: 4 main-dish servings

Tofu in Garlic-Soy Marinade

INGREDIENTS

800g extra-firm tofu

Garlic-Soy Marinade (page 29)

2 medium green bell peppers

280g uncooked long-grain
brown rice

Dilled Yogurt and Sour Cream
Sauce (page 51)

Try this entrée with Dilled Yogurt and Sour Cream Sauce (page 51) and a salad for a wonderful meal.

Soak 12 wooden skewers in water. Cut the slabs of tofu through the middle to create 4 pieces. Place each piece on a sheet of kitchen paper, cover with another sheet, and place a heavy frying pan on top to remove excess moisture. After 15 minutes, place the slabs between fresh paper to repeat the process. Cut each slab into 6 pieces to form cubes.

Place the about half of the Garlic-Soy Marinade in a shallow baking dish and add the tofu in a single layer. Pour the remainder of the marinade over the top. Marinate for about an hour, gently turning the pieces after about 30 minutes.

Meanwhile, cut the bell peppers lengthwise from the stem ends and discard the stems, membranes, and seeds. Cut the bell peppers into uniform pieces about 3cm square. Set aside.

Heat 750ml water to a boil in a medium saucepan on the hob for the rice. Stir in the rice, cover the pan, and reduce the heat to low. Cook for about 40 minutes. Remove from the heat and set aside until needed.

Preheat the barbecue to high. Using 2 skewers per serving, place them about $1^1/_2$-cm apart and start with a square of bell pepper, threading it on 2 skewers. Alternately thread the tofu and bell pepper, creating 6 threaded skewers. Reserve any residual marinade. Place the skewers on the barbecue and cook for about 20 minutes, turning several times.

To serve, mound equal amounts of rice on 6 warm serving plates and top each plate with 2 skewers. Drizzle with the reserved marinade. Serve with the Dilled Yogurt and Sour Cream Sauce if desired.

Yield: 6 main-dish servings

Cumin and
Coriander Seed-Crusted Tofu

INGREDIENTS

400g extra-firm tofu

50g cumin seed

40g coriander seed

2 tbsps (28ml) sesame oil

170g emmenthal cheese, sliced

320g fresh or frozen
   corn kernels, cooked

Salsa or dipping sauce
   (optional)

This entrée is tasty served over the cooked corn as is, but for a real treat, serve it with Smooth Tomatillo Salsa (page 38) or Barbecued Red Bell Pepper Mayonnaise (page 47) as well. I've included this recipe in the skewered chapter because the cheese-stuffed slices of tofu are held together with toothpicks even though they cook in a barbecue basket, tightly enclosing the cheese-stuffed tofu.

Cut the slab of tofu through the middle to create 2 pieces. Place each piece on a sheet of kitchen paper, cover with another sheet, and place a heavy frying pan on top to remove excess moisture. After 15 minutes, place the slabs between fresh paper to repeat the process. Cut each slab into 4 pieces, then slice the pieces in half through the middle, stacking each of the 8 pieces next to each other.

Grind together the cumin and coriander seeds in a mortar and pestle or in a seed grinder. Place the seeds on a baking sheet or cutting board in an even layer. Brush the outsides of the tofu with the sesame oil. Place the tofu pieces on top of the seeds and press to encrust them. Place an equal amount of cheese on half of the pieces and cover with the remaining pieces of tofu as you would when making a sandwich, creating 4 cheese-filled tofu steaks. Secure the halves with toothpicks.

Meanwhile, preheat the barbecue to medium-low. Place the tofu steaks in the barbecuing basket and set it on the barbecue. Grill for 3 minutes, turn carefully, and continue to barbecue for 3 more minutes.

Mound the cooked corn on 4 warm serving plates and top each serving with a tofu steak, removing the toothpicks before serving. Serve with salsa or dipping sauce if desired.

Yield: 4 main-dish servings

CHAPTER 9

Fajitas, Tacos, Burritos, and Quesadillas

This chapter is full of easy summer meals. Serve them as a quick dinner after work, or showcase several dishes for a supper party. They are easy to prepare, quick to serve, and promise to please your family and guests.

To complete the meal, serve black or refried beans and steamed rice. Season the cooked beans with cumin, coriander, mild chilli powder, a fresh bay leaf, and a bit of salt as you gently heat them through. Add some tomato juice and finely chopped serrano chillies to the rice as it cooks to give it a Tex-Mex flair. Turn to 'Salsas, Chutneys, and Dipping Sauces,' beginning on page 34, and prepare a selection of condiments to serve. If you are in a pinch for time, you may also serve your favourite commercially prepared salsas or sauces. Always set out a basket of your favourite tortilla chips.

Fajitas are the perfect choice for casual dining. They are easy to prepare and festive to serve. Buy inexpensive oval fajita pans from a Mexican specialty market or use a baking tray or cast-iron frying pan to cook the ingredients on the barbecue. If using fajita pans, you can transfer them directly to the table, placing the hot pans on tiles or trivets. If using a baking tray or frying pan, transfer the cooked ingredients to a warm serving plate. Serve the Corn, Potato, and Leek Fajitas (page 170) early in the summer, when you can still find tender leeks and fresh corn has just appeared at the market. Allow each diner to create his or her own entrée, customizing it from the ingredients you present. Serve different condiments – salsas and Guacamole (page 48) are a must – to top off the tortilla-encased bundles.

Tacos – either crisp or soft – are a delicious finger food. As with fajitas, diners can assemble their own tacos. All you do is prepare the filling and set out the crisp or soft corn tortillas and an array of condiments. Try the Tacos with Barbecued Peppers, Black Beans, and Blue Cheese (page 176) for an easy-to-prepare, casual dinner party. Serve with margaritas or ice-cold beer, tortilla chips and salsa, and a freshly sliced cantaloupe melon for a delightful meal.

Burritos are a family favourite, a humble yet flavourful offering. Some of the ingredients are barbecued in advance and then mixed with the rest of the filling. Once the burritos are placed on the barbecue, they cook quickly, so make sure the rest of the meal is ready to serve. Placing a smoker box on the barbecue yields a tasty twist to any of these recipes. We think of burritos as a simple meal, but the Refried Bean Burritos with Smoked Gouda and Spicy Tomato Sauce (page 181) or the Burritos with Spinach, Artichokes, Barbecued Red Bell Pepper, and Feta Cheese (page 182) elevate this humble fare to gourmet status. Be sure to select fresh, large, burrito-size tortillas for any of these recipes.

Quesadillas are the 'barbecued cheese sandwich' of Mexican cuisine. Quick and easy to prepare, the simple cheese quesadilla is a favourite standby lunch or light dinner offering. A flour tortilla with cheese is the standard, but adding mango, the Mexican speciality nopalito cactus, or flavourful mushrooms opens the door to gastronomic delights. Brie and Mango Quesadillas (page 184) are a delicious main course, or they can star as the opening dish for a multi-course barbecued meal.

Corn, Potato, and Leek Fajitas

INGREDIENTS

4 ears sweetcorn, not husked

2 leeks

$^1/_4$ tsp olive oil

4 red potatoes

2 tbsps (28ml) canola oil

60ml freshly squeezed lime juice

1 tbsp (14ml) honey

2 cloves garlic, finely chopped

$^1/_4$ tsp ground cumin

$^1/_4$ tsp ground coriander

$^1/_4$ tsp mild chilli powder

2 jalapeño chillies,
   seeded and diced

1 large red bell pepper, seeded
   and cut into thin strips

12 fajita-size tortillas

Guacamole (page 48)
   or prepared guacamole

Salsa Fresca (page 45)
   or prepared salsa

You must serve these fajitas with Guacamole (page 54) and a salsa such as Salsa Fresca (page 49), the vegetables will be in season early summer.

Place the corn in a plastic bag and fill the bag with water to soak the husks for about 15 minutes. Meanwhile, preheat the barbecue to high. Remove the corn from the bag of water and place the corn on the barbecue. Turn every few minutes to blacken all sides of the husks evenly. Barbecue for about 18 to 22 minutes. (The kernels will steam in the husks.) Remove the corn from the barbecue. Allow the corn to cool for a few minutes, then peel off the husks and remove the silk. Cut the kernels from the cob and set them aside.

While the corn is cooking, trim the root ends and upper green tops from the leeks. Carefully wash the leeks to remove any dirt. Cut the leeks lengthwise and brush with the olive oil. Place the leeks, cut sides down, on the barbecue and barbecue for 8 minutes. Set the leeks aside on a cutting board to cool for a few minutes and then cut into thin slices.

Meanwhile, place the potatoes in the microwave on high and cook for about 4 minutes until just soft. (They will finish cooking on the barbecue.) Remove the potatoes and set aside to cool for several minutes, then cut into bite-size cubes.

In a small bowl, whisk together the canola oil, lime juice, honey, garlic, cumin, coriander, and chilli powder. Add the jalapeño chillies and whisk to combine.

Place the leeks, potatoes, and bell pepper in a large bowl and pour the sauce over them. Gently toss to combine. Place 2 fajita pans or a large-cast iron frying pan on the barbecue and add the vegetables. Heat, turning frequently, for about 15 minutes. Wrap the tortillas in foil and place on a cool spot on the barbecue to heat through.

Transfer the vegetables and tortillas to the table and serve with your favourite guacamole and salsa.

Yield: 6 main-dish servings

Chilli, Butternut Squash,
and Onion Fajitas with Queso Fresco

INGREDIENTS

60ml olive oil

60ml freshly squeezed
   lime juice

2 cloves finely chopped garlic

$1/4$ tsp ground cumin

$1/4$ tsp ground coriander

$1/4$ tsp mild chilli powder

6 mild Anaheim chillies

455g butternut squash

2 red onions

12 fajita-size tortillas

225g crumbled queso fresco
   (can substitute cream
   cheese or ricotta)

Salsa Fresca (page 45) or
   prepared salsa

Guacamole (page 48) or
   prepared guacamole

Sour cream

This fajita is colourful and flavourful. Many varieties of long green chillies are available. I like Anaheim chillies, but you can prepare this dish with any mild or hot chilli, depending on your taste. Serve with Salsa Fresca (page 45), Guacamole (page 48), and sour cream.

In a small bowl, whisk together the olive oil, lime juice, garlic, cumin, coriander, and chilli powder. Set aside. Preheat the barbecue to high.

Remove and discard Anaheim chilli stems and scrape out the seeds for a milder dish. Cut the chillies into long strips.

Trim and discard the ends from the squashes, peel, then cut them into thick matchsticks.

Peel the onions and cut them in half. Slice the halves and separate the rings. Put the chillies, squashes, and onions in a plastic bag and drizzle with the olive-oil mixture.

Place 2 fajita pans or a large cast-iron frying pan on the barbecue and add the vegetables from the bag, drizzling all of the oil mixture over them. Heat, turning frequently, for about 15 minutes. Wrap the tortillas in foil and place on a cool spot on the barbecue to heat through.

Transfer the vegetables and tortillas to the table and serve with the queso fresco, salsa, guacamole, and sour cream.

Yield: 6 main-dish servings

Fajitas with Barbecued Squash, Refried Beans, and Fresh Squash Blossoms

INGREDIENTS

60ml canola oil

60ml freshly squeezed lime juice

6 tsps finely chopped oregano

6 assorted small summer squashes

2 onions, sliced

12 fresh squash blossoms, stems
   trimmed to about 3cm

12 fajita-size tortillas

430g tinned vegetarian
   refried beans

1 tsp crushed garlic

$1/2$ tsp cumin

$1/2$ tsp mild chilli powder

$1/4$ tsp salt

225g grated strong cheddar cheese

240g Mexican Crema
   (page 48)

225g Salsa Fresca (page 45)

The colourful ingredients in this recipe come together to create a delicious fajita. Harvest squash blossoms early in the morning from your garden, beg some from a gardening neighbour, or look for them at your local farmers' market.

In a small bowl, whisk together the canola oil, lime juice, and oregano. Set aside. Preheat the barbecue to high.

Trim the ends from the squashes and cut them into thick matchsticks. Peel the onions and cut them in half. Slice the halves and separate the rings. Put the squashes and onions in a plastic bag and drizzle with the canola-oil mixture.

Place 2 fajita pans or a large cast-iron frying pan on the barbecue and add the squashes and onions from the bag, drizzling the oil mixture remaining in the bag over them. Heat, turning frequently, for about 15 minutes. Add the squash blossoms right before you remove the fajita pans from the barbecue.

While the vegetables are cooking, wrap the tortillas in foil and place on a cool spot on the barbecue to heat through.

Meanwhile, place the refried beans in a saucepan with 60ml water. Add the garlic, cumin, chilli powder, and salt. Heat the beans over medium-low, stirring occasionally. Transfer to a serving bowl and keep warm.

Transfer the squashes and onions and tortillas to the table and serve with the refried beans, cheese, Mexican Crema, and Salsa Fresca. Allow the diners to assemble their own fajitas.

Yield: 6 main-dish servings

Tacos with BBQ Peppers, Black Beans, and Blue Cheese

INGREDIENTS

1 large red bell pepper

1 large yellow bell pepper

2 ripe Haas avocados

2 tbsps (28ml) freshly squeezed
    lime juice

430g canned black beans

4 spring onions, diced

$\frac{1}{4}$ tsp ground cumin

$\frac{1}{4}$ tsp ground coriander

$\frac{1}{2}$ tsp mild chilli powder

55g crumbled blue cheese

6 tsps finely chopped
    fresh oregano

12 standard-size corn tortillas

140g finely shredded
    green cabbage

These soft tacos are perfect to serve at a small supper barbecue. The guests can assemble their own – all you do is prepare the ingredients and set the table. Serve with steamed rice and Smooth Tomatillo Salsa (page 38). Save any left-overs and use them as an omelette filling the following day. Haas avocados have pebbled dark green or black skins.

Preheat the barbecue to high. Place the bell peppers directly on the barbecue and cook for 10 to 15 minutes, turning frequently. Cook until the skins are charred black. Transfer the peppers to a plastic or paper bag, close the bag, and set aside for about 15 minutes. When the peppers are cool enough to handle, peel off the charred skin, discard the seeds, stems, and white membranes, and cut into narrow strips. Place the strips in a bowl.

Cut the avocados in half lengthwise and remove the pits. With the avocados still in the skin, use the tip of a sharp knife to cut into cubes. Use a spoon to scoop the cubes into the bowl with the peppers. Drizzle with the lime juice and toss gently to combine. Add the black beans and spring onions and toss again.

Combine the cumin, coriander, and chilli powder in a small bowl and sprinkle over the pepper mixture. Toss to combine. Crumble the blue cheese and oregano over the pepper mixture and toss well to combine.

Place the tortillas in foil and warm them on the barbecue. Transfer the pepper mixture, tortillas, and green cabbage to the table and allow diners to fill their own tacos.

Yield: 6 main-dish servings

Soft Tacos with
Barbecued Tofu and Pickled Jalapeños

INGREDIENTS

400g extra-firm tofu

3 tbsps (45ml) canola oil

1 medium yellow onion, diced

2 cloves garlic, finely chopped

1 tsp ground cumin

1 tsp mild chilli powder

1 tsp finely chopped
   fresh oregano

$1/8$ tsp black pepper

185g tomato sauce

3 tsps finely chopped pickled
   jalapeño chillies

2 medium tomatoes, diced

12 corn tortillas

140g finely shredded
   green cabbage

Serve these delicious tacos accompanied by Peach and Pineapple Salsa with Fresh Tarragon (page 42) and Mexican Crema (page 48) for a real taste treat. If time is tight, serve with your favourite commercially prepared salsa and sour cream.

Preheat the barbecue to medium-high with a smoker box in place. Drain the tofu and cut the slabs in half width-wise. Place the tofu on a sheet of kitchen paper, cover with another sheet, and weigh down with a heavy frying pan to press out most of the moisture. Again, cut the slabs in half width-wise and brush each side with 1 tbsp of the canola oil. Place the tofu on a barbecue tray and then on the hot barbecue. Barbecue for about 10 minutes, turning several times. Remove the tofu from the barbecue and set aside to cool slightly.

Meanwhile, place the remaining 2 tbsps canola oil in a cast-iron frying pan over medium-high heat on the hob and add the onion, garlic, cumin, chilli powder, oregano, and black pepper. Sauté for about 2 minutes, then add the tomato sauce and jalapeño chillies. Crumble the barbecued tofu and add to the frying pan. Stir to incorporate and continue to cook for about 5 minutes.

Place the tortillas in foil and warm them on the barbecue. Transfer the tofu mixture, tortillas, and green cabbage to the table and allow diners to fill their own tacos.

Yield: 6 main-dish servings

Barbecued Tomatillo
and Potato Tacos with Cheese

INGREDIENTS

700g tomatillos, in the husk

455g red potatoes

2 poblano chillies, seeded and
chopped (can substitute
anaheim chillies)

60ml canola oil

1 tsp mild chilli powder

$1/2$ tsp cumin

$1/2$ tsp salt

225g grated mild cheddar cheese

140g finely shredded green cabbage

60g Mexican Crema (page 48)

12 crisp taco shells

These tacos are brimming with flavour and are a visual delight. Serve Guacamole (page 48), salsa, and tortilla chips as an appetizer, and with White Corn with Chilli Butter (page 94), to complete the meal. Prepare fresh Mexican Crema (page 48) or use a commercially prepared variety. You can also substitute sour cream if you wish.

Place the tomatillos, still in their husks, in a plastic bag and fill the bag with water. Seal and allow the tomatillos to soak for about 15 minutes.

Preheat the barbecue to high with a smoker box in place. Remove the tomatillos from the bag and place them on the barbecue. Grill for 15 to 18 minutes, turning frequently. (The husks will char slightly, but should not totally blacken.) Remove the husks and chop the tomatillos. Set aside in a bowl.

Meanwhile, cut the red potatoes into cubes and place them, along with the poblano chillies, in a plastic bag.

In a small bowl, whisk together the canola oil, chilli powder, cumin, and salt. Drizzle over the potatoes and poblano chillies. Seal the bag, allowing some of the air to remain. Toss gently to coat the potatoes and poblano chillies evenly.

Place 2 fajita pans or a cast-iron frying pan on the barbecue and add the potatoes mixture from the bag. Cook for 8 to 10 minutes, turning frequently. Add the tomatillos and toss to combine.

Place the tomatillo mixture, cheese, green cabbage, Mexican Crema, and taco shells on the table and allow diners to fill their own tacos.

Yield: 6 main-dish servings

Black Bean and
Mixed Cheese Burritos

400g tinned black beans

$1/2$ tsp crushed garlic

$1/4$ tsp ground cumin

$1/4$ tsp ground coriander

$1/4$ tsp salt

I jalapeño chilli, seeded and finely
  chopped

4 burrito-size flour tortillas

225g grated mild cheddar cheese
  and red leicester cheese

2 tbsps (28ml) canola oil

I avocado, seeded, peeled,
  and sliced

Salsa Fresca (page 49)

Corn chips

The flavourful black beans and melted cheese in this recipe make an outstanding burrito. Serve with corn chips and Salsa Fresca (page 45).

Drain the black beans, reserving about 2 tbsps of the liquid. Place the beans in a blender with the reserved liquid, garlic, cumin, coriander, salt, and jalapeño chilli. Puree until chunky-smooth.

Preheat the barbecue to medium-high. Working with one tortilla at a time, place one-quarter of the beans slightly off-centre and top with one-quarter of the cheese. Fold up the bottom end, then roll the sides to close. Set aside, seam side down.

Place 2 fajita pans or a large cast-iron frying pan or baking tray directly on the barbecue and coat with the oil. Place the burritos on the pans, frying pan, or tray, seam sides down. Cook for about 3 minutes, turn, and continue to cook for 3 minutes until nicely browned on each side. Top with the avocado and serve immediately, passing Salsa Fresca and corn chips.

Yield: 4 main-dish servings

Barbecued Vegetable
and Rice Burritos

INGREDIENTS

- 90g uncooked long-grain brown rice
- 2 medium onions
- 2 tbsps (28ml) olive oil
- 3 medium courgettes
- 2 red bell peppers
- 6 burrito-size flour tortillas
- 2 tbsps (28ml) freshly squeezed lime juice
- 1 tbsp (14ml) canola oil
- 1 tsp finely chopped chipotle chillies in adobo
- 100g shredded red cabbage

The barbecued vegetables and chipotle chilli lend a delicate smoky flavour to this dish. Chipotle chillies in adobo can be found in ethnic food shops, or online at www.coolchile.co.uk. If you like things spicy, double the amount of chillies.

Bring 235ml water to a boil in a small saucepan. Add the rice and return to a boil. Reduce the heat to very low, cover the pan, and cook for 45 minutes. Remove the saucepan from the heat and set aside, leaving the lid in place.

Meanwhile, preheat the barbecue to high with a smoker box in place. Trim off and discard the ends of the onions and peel. Cut the onions in half crosswise and lightly brush the cut sides with some of the olive oil. Place the onions on the barbecue, cut sides down. Cover and grill for about 35 minutes, turning every 8 to 10 minutes. (The onions are done when they are soft and slightly charred.)

While the onions are cooking, remove and discard the ends from the courgettes and cut them lengthwise into 3 strips. Cut the bell peppers in half, discard the stems, seeds, and white membranes, and then slice each half into thirds lengthwise. Place the courgettes and bell peppers in a plastic bag and drizzle with the remaining olive oil. Twist the bag to seal, allowing some air to remain in the bag. Toss gently to coat the vegetables evenly. Remove the courgettes and peppers from the bag, place on the barbecue, and barbecue for 15 to 20 minutes, turning several times while cooking. (They will char slightly and become limp.)

While the vegetables are cooking, wrap the tortillas in foil and place them on a cool spot on the barbecue to heat through.

Remove all of the vegetables from the barbecue and allow them to cool slightly, then coarsely chop them. Place the vegetables in a medium bowl and add the rice. Toss to combine. Add the lime juice, canola oil, and chipotle chillies to the bowl and toss to combine.

Just before serving, lay the tortillas flat on individual warmed serving plates. Evenly divide the barbecued vegetable mixture and cabbage among the tortillas. Fold the ends of each tortilla over the filling and roll closed. Serve immediately.

Yield: 6 main-dish servings

Refried Bean Burritos
with Smoked Gouda and Spicy Tomato Sauce

INGREDIENTS

430g tinned refried beans

115g sour cream

1 tsp mild chilli powder

$1/4$ tsp cumin

$1/4$ tsp coriander

$1/4$ tsp salt

6 burrito-size flour tortillas

225g grated smoked Gouda cheese

2 tbsps (28ml) canola oil

2 tbsps (30g) spicy tomato sauce

Mexican Crema (page 48) or sour
    cream (optional)

This is a fast and easy burrito to prepare, since it calls for commercially prepared spicy tomato sauce or enchilada sauce. There are many varieties available, found in ethnic food shops.

Place the refried beans in a blender or food processor with the sour cream and 30 to 60ml water. Pulse to combine. Add the chilli powder, cumin, coriander, and salt. Puree until blended to a thick (but not watery) consistency.

Preheat the barbecue to medium-high. Working with one tortilla at a time, place one-sixth of the beans slightly off-centre and top with one-sixth of the cheese. Fold up the bottom end, then roll the sides to close. Set aside, seam side down.

Place 2 fajita pans or a large cast-iron frying pan or baking tray directly on the barbecue and coat with the canola oil. Place the burritos on the pans, frying pan, or tray, seam sides down. Cook for about 3 minutes, turn, and continue to cook for 3 minutes, until nicely browned on each side. Brush the sauce evenly over the burritos, turn, and continue to cook for a minute or so. Serve the burritos immediately with Mexican Crema (page 48) or sour cream, if desired.

Yield: 6 main-dish servings

Burritos with Spinach,
Artichokes, Barbecued Red Bell Pepper, and Feta Cheese

INGREDIENTS

1 large red bell pepper

90g uncooked long-grain
    white rice

15g finely chopped fresh
    flat-leaf parsley

1 tbsp (14ml) olive oil

170g jar of water-packed
    artichoke hearts

700g fresh spinach

3 tsps finely chopped fresh
    marjoram leaves

6 burrito-size flour tortillas,
    at room temperature

115g crumbled feta cheese

2 tbsps (28ml) canola oil

These burritos have an unconventional filling that yields a delicious dish. Serve with a salad and some tortilla chips and salsa.

Preheat the barbecue to high. Place the bell pepper directly on the barbecue and grill for 10 to 15 minutes, turning frequently. (The skin will be charred black.) Transfer the pepper to a plastic bag, close the bag, and set aside for about 15 minutes. When the pepper is cool enough to handle, peel off the charred skin and discard the seeds, stems, and white membrane. Dice the pepper and set aside.

Bring 235ml water to a boil in a medium saucepan on the hob. Stir in the white rice, parsley, and olive oil. Cover, reduce the heat to very low, and cook 20 minutes. Remove the saucepan from the heat and set aside, leaving the lid in place.

Drain the artichoke hearts and cut them into bite-size pieces.

Carefully wash the spinach, discarding the stems. Pile the spinach into a saucepan, place on the hob, cover, and cook over medium heat until the spinach wilts, about 5 minutes. Drain the spinach in a colander, pressing with a wooden spoon to remove as much water as possible. Transfer the spinach to a cutting board and coarsely chop. Return the spinach to the warm saucepan, along with the artichoke hearts, barbecued bell pepper, marjoram, and cooked rice. Stir to combine.

Working with one tortilla at a time, place one-sixth of the spinach mixture slightly off-centre and top with one-sixth of the cheese. Fold up the bottom end, then roll the sides to close. Set aside, seam side down.

Place 2 fajita pans or a large cast-iron frying pan or baking tray on the barbecue and coat with the canola oil. Place the burritos on the pans, frying pan, or tray, seam sides down. Cook for about 3 minutes, turn, and continue to cook for 3 minutes, until nicely browned on each side. Serve immediately.

Yield: 6 main-dish servings

Mushroom and Cheese Quesadillas

INGREDIENTS

1 medium serrano chilli

$^1/_2$ tsp cumin seed

225g button mushrooms

$^1/_2$ medium onion, sliced

$^1/_4$ tsp salt

120ml Vegetable Stock (page 23)

1 tbsp (14ml) dry sherry

4 standard-size flour tortillas

115g grated mild cheddar cheese

Salsa (optional)

Mexican Crema (page 48)
  (optional)

This flavourful mushroom mixture is delicious melted with cheese in quesadillas. Serve with Smooth Tomatillo Salsa (page 38) and Mexican Crema (page 48) or your favourite salsa.

Remove and discard the stems of the serrano chilli; scrape out the seeds and membrane for a milder dish. Finely mince the chilli and set aside.

Crush the cumin with a mortar and pestle. Set aside.

Brush or wipe any loose dirt particles from the mushrooms and thinly slice them.

Place the mushrooms, onion, serrano chilli, and cumin in a frying pan or sauté pan that has a tight-fitting lid. Sprinkle with the salt and pour in the Vegetable Stock. Place the frying pan on the hob, cover, and cook over medium heat for 10 minutes. Remove the lid, and continue to stir and cook if more than a tbsp of liquid remains in the pan. When the mixture is fairly dry, turn off the heat and stir in the sherry. Set aside.

Meanwhile, preheat the barbecue to medium-high. Place the tortillas on a work surface and distribute one-eighth of the cheese on half of each tortilla. Distribute the mushroom mixture equally over the cheese on each tortilla, then top the mushrooms with the remaining cheese. Fold the tortillas in half, enclosing the filling. Place the quesadillas directly on the barbecue and barbecue for about 8 minutes, carefully turning several times so the cheese melts and the tortillas get barbecue marks but do not burn. Serve immediately with salsa and Mexican Crema (page 48), if desired.

Yield: 4 main-dish servings

Brie and Mango Quesadillas

INGREDIENTS

4 standard-size flour tortillas

225g brie, thinly sliced

I ripe mango, peeled, pitted, and chopped

Mango and Papaya Salsa with Jalapeños (page 37) or prepared salsa

This may sound like an unusual combination, but the flavours combine to create a delicious quesadilla. This is also a tasty appetizer for eight people. Serve with Mango and Papaya Salsa with Jalapeños (page 37).

Preheat the barbecue to medium-high. Lie the tortillas on a work surface. Place several slices of brie on half of each tortilla. Top with equal amounts of mango. Place the remaining slices of brie over the mango and fold the tortilla in half, enclosing the filling. Place the quesadillas directly on the barbecue and barbecue for about 8 minutes, carefully turning several times so the cheese melts and the tortillas get barbecue marks but do not burn. Serve immediately with Mango and Papaya Salsa with Jalapeños or prepared salsa.

Yield: 4 main-dish servings

Nopalito and Tomato Quesadillas

INGREDIENTS

225g fresh nopales

2 plum tomatoes

1 large poblano or
   anahiem chilli

1 tsp cumin seed

1 tbsp (28ml) canola oil

2 spring onions, finely chopped

1 clove garlic, finely chopped

$1/2$ tsp salt

6 standard-size flour tortillas

170g crumbled queso fresco
   (can substitute cream
   cheese or ricotta)

Salsa Fresca (page 45)

If you are lucky enough to have access to a prickly pear cactus, select a fresh, bright green paddle and try this recipe. When they are cut, the paddles – nopales – have a slimy quality similar to that of okra. This cooks away to yield a flavour that is a cross between lime and green beans. Serve these quesadillas with White Corn with Chilli Butter (page 94) for a delightful meal.

The thorns of the nopales are lodged under the small bumps that irregularly dot the paddles, use the dull edge of a knife blade to scrape off the thorns, taking care not to prick yourself. Do not remove the peel, however. Lay the nopales flat on a work surface and then cut off and discard $1^1/2$cm of the outer rim and the base end. Slice the paddles lengthwise into $^3/4$-cm strips, then cut the strips into 3cm pieces. Place the nopales in a saucepan and cover with water. Bring to a boil on the hob, reduce the heat to medium-high, cover the pan, and cook for about 15 minutes, until fork-tender. Drain the nopales in a colander and rinse well with cold water. Pat dry with paper towels and set aside.

Meanwhile, chop the tomatoes and place in a bowl. Remove and discard the stem, seeds, and membrane from the chilli. Finely dice it and add to the bowl. Add the cooked nopales and toss to combine.

Crush the cumin with a mortar and pestle.

Heat the canola oil over medium heat in a heavy frying pan. Stir in the cumin, spring onions, and garlic and sauté for 1 to 2 minutes. Add the tomato mixture and the salt. Increase the heat to medium-high and cook, stirring occasionally, for about 10 minutes, until all the liquid has evaporated.

Preheat the barbecue to medium-high. Place the tortillas on a work surface. Distribute equal amounts of the tomato mixture on half of each tortilla. Sprinkle with equal amounts of the queso fresco and fold the tortillas in half, enclosing the filling. Place the quesadillas directly on the barbecue and barbecue for about 8 minutes, carefully turning several times so the cheese melts and the tortillas get barbecue marks but do not burn. Serve immediately with Salsa Fresca (page 45).

Yield: 6 main-dish servings

CHAPTER 10

Wraps, Sandwiches, and Burgers

We all need convenience foods that we can quickly prepare, take for lunch, or eat on the run. The recipes here fit that bill. There are many variations of the wrap, sandwich, or burger, but all have in common tasty ingredients encased in leavened or flat bread and presented to eat without a fork or knife. These stuffed or layered casual meals are sometimes messy, but they're always satisfying.

Wraps are easy to make and transport well – they are the perfect meal-on-the-go. Most of the filling ingredients can be prepared ahead of time, and then encased in the wrap when ready to serve or to pack as a week-day lunch. Wraps make a delicious lunch or light supper. The Lovash with Barbecued Peppers and Eggplant (page 192) is a great recipe to serve as part of a buffet, or to take to a party. The pinwheel slices are easy to eat and transport well. Tightly wrap any left-overs and refrigerate them to be enjoyed the next day.

Everyone loves a sandwich, and adding barbecued ingredients or barbecuing the whole thing makes the everyday sandwich even more delicious. Barbecued Tomato and Cheese Sandwiches (page 194) or Barbecued Cheese Sandwiches with Cremini Mushrooms (page 201) are simple to prepare but worthy of gourmet status. Focaccia buns are the perfect shape for barbecued portobello mushrooms or barbecued egg-plant. Invite some friends over mid-week for Barbecued Eggplant on Focaccia (page 196) or Focaccia with Barbecued Portobello Mushrooms (page 195) for an easy but delicious barbecued dinner. Serve with a simple salad and chilled wine and dine alfresco.

The burger is revered; there is something universal about putting a barbecued patty of some sort on a bun with lettuce and tomato slices. Pass your favourite mustards and mayonnaise. Add sweet or tart pickles or relish and enjoy! The Barbecued Tempeh Burgers (page 202) are certain to become a family favourite.

Anaheim Chilli
and Curry Tofu Wrap

INGREDIENTS

6 Anaheim chillies (or other large
   mild green chillies)

6 chapatis or whole wheat tortillas

400g firm tofu

3 spring onions, finely chopped

80g mayonnaise

4g finely chopped fresh coriander

2 tsps curry powder

2 tsps freshly squeezed lime juice

$1/4$ tsp salt

Tofu will take on any flavour, and pairing it with curry spices is a great combination. Serve this with sliced raw vegetables for a nice lunch or serve with cucumber salad and Summer Squashes with Lemon Basil (page 93) as a dinner entrée.

Preheat the barbecue to high. Place the Anaheim chillis on the barbecue and grill for 8 to 10 minutes, turning frequently. (The skins will blacken.) Remove the chillies from the barbecue and place in a plastic bag. Seal the bag and set aside to cool. When the chillies are cool enough to handle, remove the blackened skin and place the chillies lengthwise on a cutting board, removing and discarding the stem end and seeds. Set the chillies aside.

Wrap the chapatis (a type of Indian flat bread) or tortillas in foil and place on the cooling barbecue for about 10 minutes, leaving them there until needed so they stay warm.

Meanwhile, cut the tofu into $1^1/2$-cm slices and place the slices on a sheet of kitchen paper and cover with another sheet. Place a heavy frying pan on top to press the excess water from the tofu. After 15 minutes, place the tofu slices between fresh paper and repeat the process. Crumble the tofu into a bowl. Mix in the spring onions, mayonnaise, coriander, curry powder, lime juice, and salt.

Place a warm chapati or tortilla on a work surface and place one chilli just off centre on the bread. Use a spoon to mound one-sixth of the tofu mixture on top of the chilli. Fold up the bottom and fold in the sides, then roll up tightly. Fill the remaining chapatis or tortillas in the same manner. Serve immediately or individually wrap tightly in plastic or waxed paper to enjoy later.

Yield: 6 main-dish servings

Lovash with Barbecued Peppers
and Aubergine

INGREDIENTS

2 medium aubergines

2 tbsps (30g)
   coarse salt

60mls olive oil

4 large red bell peppers

455g cream cheese,
   at room temperature

260g Basil Pesto (page 23)

3 tbsps (45ml) freshly squeezed
   lemon juice

3 rounds fresh lovash bread or
   crisp rounds, softened

100g pitted and chopped
   kalamata olives

240g baby spinach leaves

Lavash is Armenian cracker bread, and comes as tea-towel sized pieces sold in see-through packets in major supermarkets and ethnic food shops. This recipe is a great one to make ahead of time to serve as part of the meal for a small gathering of friends. Served as an appetizer, and figure about 22 to 24 servings. This can be prepared 1 day ahead.

Preheat the barbecue to medium-high. Cut off and discard the stem and bottom ends of the aubergines but do not peel them. Cut the aubergines crosswise into slices about $1^1/_2$-cm thick. To remove the aubergines' bitter juices, sprinkle both sides of the slices with the salt and place the slices on a rack to for about 30 minutes. (The salt will cause the aubergine to 'sweat' and release the bitter juices.) Rinse the aubergine slices briefly and blot them dry with kitchen paper.

   Brush each side of the aubergine slices with the olive oil and place them on the barbecue. Grill for 5 to 8 minutes until browned, turn, and continue to grill for another 5 to 8 minutes. (The slices should be tender-crisp, not mushy.) Remove the aubergine from the barbecue and set aside. When the aubergine is cool enough to handle, peel the off the skin from each slice.

   Meanwhile, place the bell peppers directly on the barbecue and barbecue for 10 to 15 minutes, turning frequently. (The pepper skin will be charred black.) Transfer the peppers to a plastic bag, close the bag, and set aside for about 15 minutes. When the peppers are cool enough to handle, peel off the charred skins and discard the seeds, stems, and white membrane. Cut the peppers into long thin strips and set aside.

   Place the cream cheese, Basil Pesto, and lemon juice in a food processor. Pulse to combine.

   Working with one round at a time, place the lovash bread on a work surface and spread one-third of the cream cheese mixture evenly over the surface with a spatula, leaving about a 12-cm rim on one edge. Cover with one-third of the aubergine and bell pepper slices. Evenly distribute one-third of the kalamata olives over the aubergine and bell peppers. Cover with one-third of the spinach leaves. Begin at the end covered with the filling and tightly roll up the lovash bread toward the uncovered edge. (The filling will move forward slightly as you roll, filling the 12-cm rim.) Wrap the rolls in plastic or waxed paper, seam sides down, and refrigerate for several hours. Repeat with the remaining lovash bread and ingredients.

   Before serving, remove the plastic or waxed paper and slice the rolls into 3-cm rounds. Arrange on a platter and serve.

Yield: 14 main-dish servings

Barbecued Tomato and Cheese Sandwiches

INGREDIENTS

2 medium tomatoes

8 slices whole wheat bread

340g sliced mozzarella cheese

40g loosely packed chiffonaded basil (see page 16 for this technique)

2 tbsps (28g) butter, melted

This sandwich is best prepared in the summer, when fresh garden tomatoes are at their peak. You will have a few more slices of tomatoes than you need for the sandwiches, so use them to garnish the serving plates.

Preheat the barbecue to medium. Core the tomatoes and slice them into 3/4-cm slices.

Place the bread on a work surface. Cover each slice with equal amounts of mozzarella cheese. Top half of them with equal amounts of tomato and sprinkle with the basil. Top with the other cheese-covered slices of bread, cheeses side down. Use a pastry brush to lightly coat the outer sides of the bread with the butter. Place the sandwiches on the barbecue and barbecue for 4 to 5 minutes, then turn and barbecue for 3 to 4 more minutes. Slice in half and serve immediately.

Yield: 4 main-dish servings

Barbecued Artichoke Panini

INGREDIENTS

1 soft-crusted baguette or 4 soft rolls

225g Provolone cheese, sliced

170g jarred marinated artichoke hearts, drained and sliced

50g chopped kalamata olives

4 pepperoncini peppers, sliced

24 basil leaves

The ingredients remind me of Italy, hence the name. Serve a crisp white wine for a casual lunch with friends while you dream of travel plans.

Preheat the barbecue to medium-high. Cut the baguette into 4 equal pieces and slice each in half, or, if using soft rolls, slice them in half. On the bottom of each slice, place one-eighth of the Provolone cheese and equal amounts of the artichoke hearts, kalamata olives, pepperoncini peppers, and basil leaves. Top with equal amounts of the remaining cheese and cover with the top of the baguette or roll. Place the sandwiches in a barbecue basket, clamp it closed, and place directly on the barbecue. Barbecue for 2 to 3 minutes, turn, and barbecue for 2 to 3 more minutes. (The cheese will melt and the bread lightly toasted.) Serve immediately.

Yield: 4 main-dish servings

Focaccia with
Barbecued Portobello Mushrooms

This has become a classic vegetarian 'burger,' and rightly so. It is delicious! You may serve this tasty mushroom on a whole wheat bun, if you prefer.

INGREDIENTS

4 large portobello mushrooms

60ml olive oil

2 tsps crushed garlic

Pinch salt

4 focaccia buns

4 butter lettuce leaves

350g Barbecued Red Bell Pepper
Mayonnaise (page 47)

Trim the stem end from each mushroom so it is flush with the gills.

Whisk together the olive oil, garlic, and salt in a small bowl. Brush the bottom of the mushrooms with some of the oil mixture, then place the mushrooms on a plate, gill sides up. Pour equal amounts of the oil mixture into the gills of each mushroom. Use a pastry brush to distribute the garlic throughout the gills, as some of it will settle in the bottom of the bowl. Set the mushrooms aside for about 15 minutes to let them absorb the oil and garlic.

Meanwhile, preheat the barbecue to high, then reduce the heat to medium-high. Place the mushrooms on the barbecue, bottom sides down. Grill for about 10 minutes, then turn and continue to grill for about 10 more minutes.

Slice the focaccia buns in half and place them cut sides down on the barbecue to toast for a minute or two.

To serve, place the focaccia buns on individual plates and top each one with a mushroom and lettuce leaf. Serve with the Barbecued Red Bell Pepper Mayonnaise.

Yield: 4 main-dish servings

BBQ Aubergine
on Focaccia

I like this on a focaccia bun, but you may use a whole wheat or sourdough bun. The Remoulade Sauce really makes this a spectacular sandwich.

INGREDIENTS

1 medium aubergine

1 tbsp (15g) coarse salt

2 large tomatoes, cored and sliced

2 tbsps (28ml) olive oil

4 focaccia buns

4 butter lettuce leaves

75g Remoulade Sauce (page 53)

Cut off and discard the stem and bottom ends of the aubergine and slice crosswise into 4 slices about 3-cm thick. To remove the aubergine's bitter juices, sprinkle both sides of the slices with the salt and place them on a rack for about 30 minutes. (The salt will cause the aubergine to 'sweat' and release the bitter juices.) Briefly rinse the slices and blot them dry with kitchen paper.

Remove and discard the stem ends from the tomatoes and cut them into 8 thick slices. Set aside.

Meanwhile, preheat the barbecue to medium-high. Brush each side of the aubergine slices with the olive oil and place them on the grill. Barbecue for 7 to 9 minutes until browned, turn, and continue to barbecue for another 7 to 9 minutes.

Slice the focaccia buns in half and place them cut sides down on the barbecue to toast for a minute or two.

To serve, place the focaccia buns on individual plates and top each one with an aubergine slice and tomato slices. Top with a lettuce leaf and serve with the Remoulade Sauce.

Yield: 4 main-dish servings

Japanese Aubergine
and Red Bell Pepper Sandwich with Pesto

INGREDIENTS

2 medium red bell peppers

2 Japanese aubergines

3 tbsps (45ml olive oil

4 sweet rolls

175g Basil Pesto (page 23) or
   prepared pesto

1 medium tomato, sliced

2 ounces (55g) thinly shaved
   Parmesan cheese

All of the ingredients for this sandwich are at the peak of the season during the summer. Prepare fresh Basil Pesto (page 23) or use a commercially prepared pesto. Enjoy this sandwich for lunch or for a casual dinner served with a salad.

Preheat the barbecue to medium-high. Cut the bell peppers in half lengthwise, discarding the stems, seeds, and white membrane. Cut each half in two to create 8 slices. Set aside.

Remove and discard the stem end from the aubergines and cut them lengthwise into $^3/_4$-cm strips. Place the aubergines in a plastic bag with the olive oil and toss to coat evenly.

Place the bell peppers on the barbecue and grill for about 5 minutes per side until they soften but do not char, turning frequently. Remove the peppers from the barbecue and set aside. Remove the aubergine from the bag, place on the barbecue, and cook for about 2 minutes per side. (The aubergine will soften and get barbecue marks but should not char.)

Slice the sweet rolls in half and coat each side with equal amounts of Basil Pesto or prepared pesto. Layer an equal amount of the barbecued bell pepper and aubergine on the bottom side of each bun. Add the tomato and Parmesan cheese, then cover with the top of the bun. Place the sandwiches in a barbecue basket and heat through for about 2 minutes, turning once. Serve immediately.

Yield: 4 main-course servings

Sweet Rolls
with Barbecued Peppers and Endive

INGREDIENTS

1 large bulb garlic

1/4 tsp olive oil

2 medium red bell peppers

2 Anaheim chillies (or other large
  mild green chillies)

4 sweet rolls

175g Barbecued Red Bell Pepper
  Mayonnaise (page 47)

8 slices Edam cheese

2 small Belgium endives,
  separated into leaves

8 marinated sun-dried tomatoes

This is a delightful summertime sandwich, quick to prepare on the barbecue. You may also duplicate it during the winter months if you live in an area where a variety of fresh peppers are available, by barbecuing the produce on an indoor barbecue.

Preheat the barbecue to medium. Rub the papery skin from the garlic, but do not break into individual cloves. Cut about 1^1/$_2$cm off the pointed top end of the bulb and rub the cut surface with the olive oil. Place the garlic, cut side up, in a covered clay or glass baking dish and place on the barbecue. (You can wrap it in foil. Then place the foil packet on a baking stone or on baking bricks so the garlic cooks but does not burn on the bottom.) Barbecue the garlic for about 45 minutes. When the garlic feels very soft when gently squeezed, remove from the barbecue. Set aside and cool for several minutes. When the garlic is cool enough to handle, squeeze the garlic paste from the cloves into a small bowl.

Cut the bell peppers in half lengthwise, discarding the stems, seeds, and white membrane. Cut each half in two to create 8 slices.

Cut each Anaheim chilli from the stem to create 8 slices, discarding the stems and seeds. Place the bell peppers and Anaheim chillies on the barbecue and barbecue for about 2 minutes per side, until they soften but do not char. Remove the peppers and chillies from the barbecue and set aside.

Slice the sweet rolls in half. Spread the barbecued garlic evenly on the bottom side of each roll. Apply the Barbecued Red Bell Pepper Mayonnaise to the top sides. Layer the Edam cheese, barbecued bell peppers, barbecued Anaheim chillies, endive, and sun-dried tomatoes on the garlic side of the roll. Cover with the top of the roll and serve.

Yield: 4 main-dish servings

Tofu 'BLT' Sandwich

INGREDIENTS

400g extra-firm tofu

2 tbsps (28ml) toasted sesame oil

12 slices sourdough bread

2 tbsps (28g) butter, melted

120g mayonnaise

2 tbsps (30g) Dijon mustard

3 medium tomatoes, thinly sliced

1/2 tsp salt

Several grinds black pepper,
   to taste

6 butter lettuce leaves

This 'BLT' (or perhaps it should be called a 'TLT') features barbecued tofu that is smoked with wood chips as it barbecues. It will become one of your favourites.

Preheat the barbecue to high with a smoker box in place. Cut the slab of tofu through the middle to create 2 pieces. Place each piece on a sheet of kitchen paper and cover with another sheet. Place a heavy frying pan on top to press the excess water from the tofu. After 15 minutes, place the slabs between fresh paper and repeat the process. Cut the tofu into 12 thin slices. Brush each side of tofu with the sesame oil and place the slices on the barbecue. Barbecue for 6 to 7 minutes, turn, and barbecue for 6 to 7 more minutes.

Evenly coat one side of each slice of bread with the butter. Place the bread, buttered sides down, on the barbecue and barbecue for about 2 minutes, until the bread is toasted and shows barbecue marks. Place the bread on a work surface, barbecued sides down. Coat half of the slices with equal amounts of mayonnaise and the remaining slices with mustard. Place equal amounts of the barbecued tofu on the mustard-coated slices. Top the tofu with the tomato, salt, and black pepper. Cover with lettuce leaves and the mayonnaise-coated slice of bread. Cut the sandwiches in half and serve immediately.

Yield: 6 main-dish servings

Barbecued Cheese Sandwiches
with Cremini Mushrooms

INGREDIENTS

2 tbsps (28ml) olive oil

2 tsps crushed garlic

570g cremini mushrooms

8 slices sourdough
sandwich bread

2 tbsps (30g) Dijon mustard

16 slices Provolone cheese
(about 225g)

2 tbsps (28g) unsalted
butter, melted

Everyone loves barbecued cheese sandwiches, but this version is a gourmet delight. Barbecuing the mushrooms and then placing them inside the sandwiches creates a wonderful flavour.

Preheat the barbecue to medium. Place the olive oil and garlic in a bowl and whisk together to combine. Place the mushrooms in a bag and drizzle the olive oil mixture over them. Twist the bag to seal, allowing some air to remain in the bag. Toss gently to coat the mushrooms evenly. Place the mushrooms on the barbecue stem side up and grill for about 5 minutes. Turn and continue to grill for about 5 minutes. Remove the mushrooms from the barbecue and set aside. Slice the mushrooms when cool enough to handle.

Meanwhile, spread one side of each slice of bread with a thin layer of mustard. Evenly layer each slice with the Provolone cheese and then place equal amounts of the mushroom slices on one side of the bread, then top with the other slice of the bread. Use a pastry brush to lightly coat the outer sides of the bread with the butter. Place the sandwiches on the barbecue and grill for 4 to 5 minutes, turn, and grill for 3 to 4 more minutes. Slice the sandwiches in half and serve immediately.

Yield: 4 main-dish servings

Barbecued Tempeh Burgers

INGREDIENTS

2 packs soy tempeh (225g each)

60ml soy sauce

2 tbsps (28ml) canola oil

2 tbsps (28ml) dark sesame oil

4 tsps crushed garlic

6 sesame-seed buns

I large tomato, sliced

6 butter lettuce leaves

Serve this burger with your favourite condiments, such as mayonnaise, mustard, ketchup, and pickles. It has a hearty, meaty texture and flavour.

Carefully slice each piece of tempeh to create 6 thin slices.

In a small bowl, whisk together the soy sauce, canola oil, sesame oil, and garlic. Pour the mixture into a lipped baking sheet and place the tempeh on top. Marinate the tempeh for about 30 minutes, carefully turning several times.

Preheat the barbecue to medium. Place the tempeh on the barbecue and grill for 3 to 4 minutes. Carefully turn the tempeh and continue to grill for 3 to 4 more minutes.

Meanwhile, slice the sesame-seed buns in half and place them, cut sides down, on the barbecue to toast for a few minutes.

To serve, place the tempeh on one side of each bun. Allow each diner to garnish as desired with the tomato and lettuce.

Yield: 6 main-dish servings

Tofu Burgers

Serve these classic vegetarian burgers with pickles, mustard or ketchup, and mayonnaise.

INGREDIENTS

100g uncooked sushi rice

400g firm tofu

35g breadcrumbs

80g diced white onion

1 tbsp (14ml) olive oil

1 tbsp (14ml) soy sauce

1 tsps crushed garlic

1 tsp vegetarian-style
    Worcestershire sauce

1 egg, beaten

2 tbsps (28ml) canola oil

8 whole wheat buns

2 large tomatoes, sliced

1/2 head iceberg lettuce, shredded

Bring 300ml water to a boil on the hob in a saucepan, then stir in the rice. Cover, reduce the heat to very low, and cook for about 20 minutes, until the water is absorbed. Remove the saucepan from the heat and set aside, covered, for about 5 minutes.

Meanwhile, cut the tofu into 3/4-cm slices and place them on a sheet of kitchen paper. Cover with another sheet and gently press to remove as much of the moisture as possible. Crumble the tofu into a bowl. Stir in the bread crumbs, onion, olive oil, soy sauce, garlic, Worcestershire sauce, and egg. Add the rice and stir to combine. Use your hands to form into 8 patties. Set them aside on a plate.

Preheat the barbecue to high. Place 2 fajita pans or a cast-iron frying pan on the barbecue to heat. Coat with the canola oil and place the patties on to cook. Cook for about 8 minutes, turn, and continue to cook for another 8 minutes, until heated through.

Slice the buns in half and place them, cut sides down, on the barbecue to toast for a few minutes.

To serve, place the patties on one side of each bun. Allow each diner to garnish as desired with the tomatoes and lettuce.

Yield: 8 main-dish servings

CHAPTER II

Barbecued Desserts

The perfect way to end a barbecued meal is with a flavourful barbecued fruit dessert. The barbecue will still be hot enough, or it may quickly be reheated, to sear some fresh fruit to enjoy in a variety of ways. Always choose firm, ripe fruit so that it will stand up to the barbecue temperature.

Barbecued desserts are quick to prepare and to take from the barbecue to the table, so consider them even when you are not preparing a barbecued meal. Fruit from the barbecue is a delicious way to get one of those recommended fruit servings into your daily diet!

Most of these barbecued desserts are seasonal, so you will want to enjoy the particular fruit when it is at its peak. Strawberries and cherries are a sign that spring is finally here. Serve the Strawberries Soaked in Late-Harvest Riesling (page 206) with barbecued cake for an interesting twist to the traditional strawberry shortcake. Barbecued Morello Cherries and Ice Cream (page 207) will make you yearn for the first cherries of the season, as barbecuing the cherries unlocks the natural sugars and sparks the flavour.

As the season progresses, new fruits become the stars. When apricots appear, be sure to serve Barbecued Apricots with Chocolate Mousse (page 207), a guaranteed palate-pleaser. Peaches ripen next, along with nectarines. Yellow Peaches with Ginger Glaze (page 209) is sure to delight family and friends. Pears and cantaloupe are mid- to late-summer fruits. Enjoy Barbecued Red Bartlett Pears with Savoury Ricotta Cheese (page 208) and Cantaloupe with Raspberry Sorbet (page 211) with your summertime meals.

Tropical bananas and pineapples are always available, so anytime you want to fire up the barbecue, consider Barbecued Pineapple with Balsamic Vinegar and Brown Sugar (page 213) or Barbecued Bananas with Ice Cream and Chocolate (page 210). They will bring that spark of summer to the winter table.

Moist slices of cake may also be placed on the barbecue just long enough to develop barbecue marks for an interesting presentation as an accompaniment to most barbecued fruits. Feel free to substitute frozen yogurt or tofu ice cream in the recipes that call for ice cream. Have fun with the recipes in this chapter and use them to inspire your own creations.

Strawberries
Soaked in Late-Harvest Riesling

INGREDIENTS

8 large strawberries, hulled

235ml late-harvest Riesling

120ml whipping cream

1 tbsp (12g) sugar

1/4 tsp vanilla

This is a simple but lovely way to end a spring or early summer meal. Choose the largest strawberries that you can. Purchase a buttery cake and place slices on the barbecue to serve with the strawberries.

Place the strawberries in a bowl. Pour the Riesling over them and allow them to soak for about 20 minutes.

Put the whipping cream in a cold bowl and whip until soft peaks begin to form. Add the sugar and vanilla and whip to incorporate. Place in the refrigerator until needed.

When you are ready to serve, preheat the barbecue to medium. Place the whole strawberries on the barbecue. Cook for 6 to 8 minutes, turning frequently. Spoon equal portions of the whipped cream into 4 small bowls. Place 2 strawberries in each bowl and serve immediately.

Yield: 4 servings

BBQ Apricots
with Chocolate Mousse

My niece, Natalie Geiskopf, loves to create desserts. She developed this mousse recipe, which is embellished with barbecued apricots. Serve with a glass of port, if you wish.

INGREDIENTS

570g silken tofu

3 tbsps (45ml) milk

2 tbsps (25g) sugar

170g semi-sweet chocolate chips

6 large apricots

Place the tofu in a blender or food processor and add the milk and sugar. Puree until smooth.

Melt the chocolate chips in a double boiler or microwave oven. Add to the tofu mixture and puree to incorporate. Spoon the mousse into small dessert dishes and place in the refrigerator for several hours to chill.

Preheat the barbecue to medium-high. Cut the apricots in half and place them cut sides down on the barbecue. Cover the barbecue and barbecue for 5 to 7 minutes until soft. Arrange 2 halves on top of each of the 6 mousse servings.

Yield: 6 servings

Barbecued Morello Cherries
and Ice Cream

INGREDIENTS

450g firm Morello cherries

235ml late-harvest dessert wine

6 scoops organic chocolate
   ice cream

Barbecuing cherries may not be the first thought that comes to mind, but once you have tried this dessert, you will be looking forward to cherry season every year!

Stem the cherries and place them in a bowl. Pour the dessert wine over them and allow them to soak for about 15 minutes.

When you are ready to serve, preheat the barbecue to medium. Most barbecue racks are designed so that the cherries will not fall through the slats. If yours has wide openings, place the cherries in a barbecue basket or mesh rack. Barbecue for about 3 minutes, until the cherries burst. Place one scoop of ice cream on 6 individual plates and top with the cherries.

Yield: 6 servings

Nectarines
with Almond Glaze

I like the flavour of Torani Syrup, but you may use a different variety of almond-flavoured syrup or even amaretto.

INGREDIENTS

2 tbsps (28ml) almond syrup

2 tbsps (40g) honey

2 tbsps (28g) unsalted butter, melted

4 firm, ripe nectarines

8 scoops ice cream

Place the almond syrup, honey, and butter in a small bowl and mix to combine. Set aside.

When you are ready to serve, preheat the barbecue to medium. Cut the nectarines in half and remove the pits. Brush some of the almond mixture on the cut sides of the nectarines, then place the nectarines cut sides down on the barbecue. Reserve the rest of the almond mixture. Barbecue the nectarines for 5 to 8 minutes, until the juices begin to drip and the nectarines are slightly soft.

Place the barbecued nectarine halves on 8 individual serving plates with a scoop of ice cream. Drizzle with the remaining almond mixture and serve.

Yield: 8 servings

Barbecued Bartlett Pears
with Savoury Ricotta Cheese

INGREDIENTS

210g ricotta cheese

1/8 tsp cinnamon

Several grinds nutmeg, to taste

2 firm, ripe Bartlett pears

1 tbsp (14g) unsalted butter, melted

2 tbsps (40g) honey, warmed

4 sprigs fresh mint

Most Bartlett pears are the popular green-skinned types that turn golden yellow when ripe. Growers have developed a red-skinned variety that is particularly pretty — seek them out at your local farmers' market. Either variety is delicious when prepared for this dessert. Make sure the pears are firm but ripe, and not too soft.

Place the ricotta cheese in a bowl and stir in the cinnamon and nutmeg. Set aside in the refrigerator until needed.

When you are ready to serve, preheat the barbecue to medium. Cut the pears in half lengthwise and remove and discard the cores, leaving the halves intact. Use a pastry brush to coat the cut sides with the melted butter. Transfer the pears to the barbecue, cut sides down. Grill for about 4 minutes.

Place equal amounts of the ricotta cheese mixture on 4 individual serving plates. Top each with a pear half. Drizzle with the honey and garnish with the mint sprigs.

Yield: 4 servings

Yellow Peaches
with Ginger Glaze

This is an easy and elegant dessert. Choose firm yellow peaches – not ones that are ready-to-eat ripe.

INGREDIENTS

3 tsps grated fresh ginger, firmly packed

255g honey

4 firm, ripe peaches

8 scoops vanilla ice cream

Fresh mint sprigs

Place 120ml water in a small saucepan on the hob and add the ginger. Bring to a rapid simmer over medium-high heat. Add the honey and continue to cook until reduced by half, stirring occasionally. Remove the saucepan from the heat and set aside to cool. Strain to remove the ginger.

When you are ready to serve, preheat the barbecue to medium. Cut the peaches in half and remove the pits. Brush some of the ginger mixture on the cut sides of the peaches, then place the peaches cut sides down on the barbecue. Grill for 5 to 8 minutes, until juices begin to drip and the peaches are slightly soft.

Meanwhile, put the remaining ginger mixture in a small saucepan and place on the hob over medium heat. Cook to caramelize, stirring frequently. Place the barbecued peach halves on 8 individual serving plates with a scoop of ice cream. Drizzle with the ginger sauce and garnish with the mint.

Yield: 8 servings

Barbecued Bananas
with Ice Cream and Chocolate

INGREDIENTS

4 firm, ripe bananas or
  8 Manzano bananas

1 tbsp (14g)
  unsalted butter, melted

1 tbsp (14ml)
  apricot brandy

1 tbsp (20g) honey

Pinch cinnamon

Several grinds nutmeg, to taste

8 small scoops vanilla ice cream

120ml chocolate syrup

12 fresh cherries (optional)

There are many varieties of bananas in addition to the Cavendish variety that you typically find at the supermarket. If you can find the Manzano – also called finger bananas – use them, as they are especially attractive for this dish.

When you are ready to serve, preheat the barbecue to medium. Peel the bananas and cut in half lengthwise.

In a saucepan, melt the butter and add the apricot brandy, honey, cinnamon, and nutmeg. Brush the bananas with the butter mixture and place them crosswise on the barbecue or on a barbecuing grate. Barbecue for about 4 minutes, turning once.

To serve, arrange the bananas in 4 shallow dishes and top with 2 scoops of ice cream. Drizzle with the chocolate sauce. Top with the cherries, if desired.

Yield: 4 servings

Cantaloupe with Raspberry Sorbet

INGREDIENTS

- 1/2 ripe cantaloupe
- 4 scoops raspberry sorbet (or other non-citrus soft fruit sorbet)
- 4 tbsps Fresh Blueberry Sauce (page 33)
- 4 sprigs fresh mint

Cantaloupe is always good icy cold, this barbecued version brings out the natural sugars of the melon and is delicious with raspberry sorbet.

When you are ready to serve, preheat the barbecue to medium. Without peeling, cut the cantaloupe into 8 slices. Place the cantaloupe on the barbecue and grill for 2 to 3 minutes on each side. Remove from the barbecue and place 2 slices on each of the 4 serving plates. Top each serving of cantaloupe with a scoop of sorbet and a drizzle of Fresh Blueberry Sauce. Garnish with the mint.

Yield: 4 servings

Bartlett Pears
with Butterscotch

Choose firm, ripe pears for this dessert. Make the sauce ahead of time to allow it to cool. Garnish with mint sprigs and serve with biscuits.

INGREDIENTS

- 75g packed brown sugar
- 60ml light corn syrup
- 2 tbsps (28g) unsalted butter
- 60ml whipping cream
- 1/2 tsp vanilla extract
- Several grinds fresh nutmeg, to taste
- 2 firm, ripe Bartlett pears
- Mint sprigs

Place the brown sugar, corn syrup, and 1 tbsp of the butter in a small saucepan on the hob. Bring to a boil over medium heat, stirring constantly. Boil for about 1 minute and remove from the heat. Stir in the cream, vanilla, and nutmeg. Cool for at least 30 minutes before serving. (The sauce will thicken as it cools. You may refrigerate it, but bring it to room temperature before serving.)

When you are ready to serve, preheat the barbecue to medium. Cut the pears in half lengthwise and remove and discard the cores, leaving the halves intact. Melt the remaining 1 tbsp of butter and use a pastry brush to coat the cut sides of the pears. Transfer the pears to the barbecue, cut sides down. Barbecue for about 4 minutes. Remove the pears from the barbecue and place on 4 individual serving plates. Drizzle with the butterscotch sauce and serve immediately. Garnish with the mint.

Yield: 4 servings

Barbecued Plantains with
Chocolate Sauce and Almonds

INGREDIENTS

1 plantain

1 tbsp (14g) unsalted butter, melted

4 scoops vanilla ice cream

Chocolate syrup

2 tbsps (15g) chopped, dry-roasted almonds

Plantains are large green-skinned fruit that look like bananas. This member of the banana family has a more starchy texture than the common yellow Cavendish banana. It is best when cooked before serving. Try a caramel sauce or Fresh Blueberry Sauce (page 33) for a variation.

When you are ready to serve, preheat the barbecue to medium. Remove and discard the stem end of the plantain and, without peeling it, cut into 4 equal pieces. Brush the cut sides with butter and place on the barbecue. Barbecue for 5 to 6 minutes, turning several times. (The plantain will begin to caramelize, and you will smell the sweetness.) Remove the plantain from the barbecue and peel off the skin. Cut each piece in half lengthwise and place 2 halves on 4 individual serving plates. Put a scoop of ice cream on each plate and drizzle with chocolate syrup. Top with equal an amount of the almonds and serve immediately.

Yield: 4 servings

Barbecued Pineapple with
Balsamic Vinegar and Brown Sugar

INGREDIENTS

1 ripe golden pineapple

3 tbsps (45g)
  unsalted butter, melted

60ml balsamic vinegar

75g brown sugar

This is a very simple, but simply delicious, dessert. To select a ripe pineapple, look for a golden tone to the skin. Pull one of the centre leaves from the top of the pineapple. If it releases easily, the pineapple is perfectly ripe.

Place the pineapple on its side on a cutting board and cut off the top with the leaves (reserve to garnish the serving platter, if desired) and the bottom end. Set the pineapple upright and cut the rind from the fruit in lengthwise strips, slicing deep enough to remove the eyes. Cut the pineapple in half crosswise into $^3/_4$-cm thick slices. Remove the fibrous core from the centre of each slice using a sharp knife or a melon baller.

When you are ready to serve, preheat the barbecue to medium. Brush both sides of the pineapple slices with the melted butter and place on the barbecue. Grill for 4 to 6 minutes, turn, and continue to grill for about 4 minutes. Drizzle equal amounts of the balsamic vinegar over each slice and top with equal amounts of brown sugar. Continue to barbecue for 1 to 2 minutes. (The sugar will melt into the pineapple, and both sides will have barbecue marks.) Place pineapple slices on a platter with the reserved pineapple leaves in the centre or place slices on individual serving plates. Serve immediately.

Yield: 6 servings

Glossary of Specialty Ingredients

Arborio rice. This short, oval-shaped rice is the key ingredient necessary to produce the classic, creamy rice preparation called risotto. Risotto is the signature comfort-food dish of Northern Italy.

Asiago. Asiago is usually sold as an aged, dried cheese that comes in a block or grated form. It is less salty than Parmesan and has its own unique nutty flavour.

Balsamic vinegar. This vinegar is uniquely rich, with a dense yet mellow flavour. True balsamic vinegar is produced in the Italian province of Modena according to ancient techniques. It is aged for ten to fifty years in wooden barrels before bottling.

Basmati rice. This aromatic rice is primarily grown in India and Pakistan. It is available in white and brown varieties. Briefly rinse the rice before cooking for a light and fluffy texture.

Bok choy. Also called Chinese cabbage, this vegetable is used extensively in Asian cooking. The dark-green leaves are attached to thick, smooth white stems. The leaves have a slightly peppery taste; the stems are somewhat sweeter and quite succulent. Shop for baby bok choy in large supermarkets and ethnic food shops.

Broccoli rabe. Known as *cime di rapa* or *rapini* in Italy, this wild form of broccoli is prized for its sharp, bitter flavour. It resembles a very thin, leafy broccoli stalk with no pronounced head. Shop for it in Italian markets and large supermarkets.

Bulgur wheat. Bulgur is produced from whole wheat kernels. The kernels are steam-cooked, then dried and cracked into a coarse, medium, or fine grain.

Cannellini beans. These white, kidney-shaped beans have a mildly nutty flavour and hail from Tuscany. These beans may be purchased from your supermarket or in health food shops.

Chapati. This Indian flat bread looks much like a flour tortilla but is made from whole wheat flour. Use it as you would use a flour tortilla for a more nutritious wrap.

Chipotle chillies in adobo. These are smoked jalapeños that are tinned *en adobo* – in a rich sauce made from tomatoes, vinegar, and spices. They have a distinctive, smoky flavour and are quite hot, so a little goes a long way. Find these in ethnic food shops or online at www.coolchile.co.uk.

Couscous. This semolina pasta traces its roots to northern Africa. It is made from precooked semolina wheat, and the resulting tiny grains of couscous cook quickly when added to a small amount of boiling water.

Crema. This slightly soured cream is often served in Mexico as a table condiment. It is neither as sour nor as thick as standard supermarket sour cream. Shop for it in ethnic food shops or use half sour cream, half single cream.

Crème fraîche. This slightly soured cream has a semi-thick texture – but not as thick as standard sour cream – with a tart, piquant flavour. It is used extensively in Mediterranean, French, and Italian cooking.

Crostini. Crostini is an Italian word that refers to crunchy barbecued or oven-baked toasts made from slightly stale bread. Crostini is most frequently eaten with a variety of savoury toppings.

Dried tomatoes. Also referred to as sun-dried tomatoes, they have an intense flavour and a chewy texture. They are sold dried or reconstituted in olive oil. Most recipes call for the dried variety. They should be reconstituted before using in a recipe. To reconstitute sun-dried tomatoes, place them in a small bowl and cover them with water to soak for about 30 minutes, or place the bowl in the microwave for about a minute. Squeeze out most of the liquid and chop as called for in the recipe.

Endive. Also known as Belgian endive or chicory, this smooth, pale, elongated vegetable is comprised of tightly closed, creamy yellow or white leaves. The flavour is slightly bitter, and the texture is both crisp and velvety.

Fermented black beans. The fermentation of these black beans (also called turtle beans) causes them to be quite salty. They are popular in Japanese and Chinese cooking, and it is best to rinse them before using. Look for them in ethnic food shops and health food shops.

Garlic. Garlic is sold in many forms, including fresh, crushed, and granulated. Each adds a pungent punch. Fresh garlic is sold in bulbs and is baked whole to produce a paste or separated into individual cloves, peeled, and then sliced, chopped, or minced before using. Crushed garlic comes in a jar and is ready to add to a recipe in a measured amount. Granulated garlic is a dried form with a texture similar to that of coarse salt.

Greaseproof paper. Sometimes referred to as parchment paper, this heat-proof paper is used for *en papillote* cooking – the classic French meal-in-a-pouch preparation. Shop for it in supermarkets or ironmongers, usually displayed with the other standard kitchen wraps.

Jícama. Jícama has a sweet, white flesh that maintains its delectable crispness for a long time after it is cut. It is a root vegetable that has a light brown skin that is stringy and should always be stripped off before using. Water chestnuts are an acceptable substitute.

Kalamata olives. Sometimes called calamata olives, these large, succulent, purple-black olives are native to Greece. They have an intense and piquant flavour.

Lemon grass. There is no substitute for the flavour of fresh lemon grass. The outer green is stripped away from the thick grass stalk to reveal a white centre. This is finely minced or crushed before being added to a recipe. You can buy plants from herb farms and catalogues, and they're easy to grow in pots. Or shop for the stalks in ethnic food shops.

Mirin. Mirin is the sweet counterpart to sake, the Japanese rice wine. It is used extensively in Asian cooking, adding an interesting flavour note to many recipes.

Miso. Miso is a fermented soybean paste. Some varieties are intensely salty, while others have a mellow, sweeter flavour. Mild, light-coloured miso is less salty than the darker varieties; shop for it at Asian markets or natural food stores.

Nopales. Also called nopalitos, these paddles are harvested from the prickly pear cacti. They have a succulent texture and a distinctive fresh flavour with just a hint of tartness. Tinned nopalitos are also available, but the texture and flavour is not as good as that of fresh nopalitos.

Pickled jalapeños. The pickling process adds a pleasant, piquant note to this hot pepper, which is sold in jars and is readily available year-round. Shop for them in large supermarkets or ethnic food shops.

Polenta. Polenta is dried corn ground into a medium-grain meal. Ethnic food shops and health food shops sell it labeled 'polenta,' but fine-ground cornmeal can be substituted if you can't find polenta itself.

Ponzu sauce. This is a citrus-seasoned soy sauce that is delightful as a table condiment and adds a unique flavour note when used as an ingredient in a recipe. Shop for it in Asian food shops.

Portobello mushrooms. These large mushrooms can measure 12 to 18cm across. They have a good, solid, 'meaty' texture. They are widely available in grocery stores and in Italian and specialty markets.

Queso fresco. This part-skim cheese has a mild flavour and a crumbly texture. It is used primarily as a topping rather than a filling, since it does not melt smoothly. Substitute ricotta or cream cheese if need be.

Radicchio. The most common variety of this vegetable is purple, mottled with white. The small heads have a bitter flavour note, most large supermarkets carry the heads or the leaves.

Rice wine vinegar. This vinegar has a sweet yet tart flavour, and it is delicious sprinkled over raw vegetables or used as an ingredient in many sauces and salad dressings.

Sesame tahini. Tahini is ground raw or toasted sesame seeds. The resulting spread has a texture similar to smooth peanut butter. Shop for it in ethnic food shops or health food shops if your supermarket doesn't carry it.

Shiitake mushrooms. These mushrooms are available fresh or dried in Asian markets and large supermarkets. They have a rich flavour and chewy texture, so it's best to slice or chop them before using. The dried variety needs to be reconstituted before using. To reconstitute, place them in a small bowl and cover them with water to soak for about 30 minutes, or place the bowl in the microwave for about a minute. Squeeze out most of the liquid and chop as called for in the recipe.

Soba. Soba is a thin Japanese noodle typically made with buckwheat flour. For the best selection, shop for them at an Asian food shop.

Sweet chili sauce. This prepared, sweet, hot chili sauce adds a distinctive flavour when used as an ingredient in a recipe or served as a table condiment. Shop for it at Asian food shops.

Tempeh. Tempeh is produced by fermenting whole soybeans, sometimes combining them with other grains. This high-protein food is very dense and has a chewy texture with a nutty flavour.

Tofu. Tofu is made from soy milk that has been coagulated to form curds. The blandness of this high-protein food makes it very versatile, as it readily takes on the flavours paired with it. Tofu comes in various textures, from soft and silky to dense and chewy. Each variety is suitable for different types of dishes.

Tomatillos (Also known as Chinese Lanterns). Tomatillos grow inside paper husks, which is discarded before the cherry tomato-size tomatillos are cooked. They are firm in texture and lime green in colour with a tart, fresh flavour that is essential to many traditional Mexican dishes. Tinned tomatillos are also available and can be used when fresh ones aren't in season, or substitute cherry tomatoes.

Wasabi. Wasabi, a pungent green form of Asian horseradish, is commonly sold in a dry form that is mixed with water or rice wine vinegar before using. Shop for it in Asian food shops.

Index

A

Anaheim Chilli and Curry Tofu Wrap, 191

appetizers. *See* hors d'oeuvres

Apricots with Chocolate Mousse, BBQ, 207

Arborio rice, 125, 214

    See also rice

artichokes

    Barbecued Artichoke Panini, 194

    Barbecued Artichokes with Lemon Butter and Summer Savoury, 63

    Burritos with Spinach, Artichokes, Barbecued Red Bell Pepper, and Feta Cheese, 184

    Pasta with BBQ Artichokes and Fresh Shiitake Mushrooms, 134–135

    Pizza with Courgette, Artichokes, and Feta Cheese, 113

Asiago cheese, 214

asparagus

    Asparagus and Mushroom Pizza with Mustard, Dill, Mozzarella, and Feta, 109

    Asparagus Pizza, 108

    Asparagus, Shiitake Mushrooms, and Tofu en Papillote, 119

    Asparagus with Watercress Sauce, 90

    Pasta with BBQ Asparagus and Onions, 127

    Pasta with Barbecued Fennel and Asparagus, 137

    Saffron Rice with Barbecued Fennel, Asparagus, and Leeks, 141

aubergine

    Crostini with Barbecued Courgette and Aubergine, 66

    Aubergine with Ricotta and Tomato Coulis, 59

    Fusilli Pasta in Caper Cream Sauce with Barbecued Aubergine and Pepper Strips, 130

    BBQ Aubergine on Focaccia, 196

    BBQ Aubergine Parmesan with Soft Polenta, 152

    BBQ Aubergine Spread, 72

    Japanese Aubergine and Red Bell Pepper Sandwich with Pesto, 197

    Lavash with Barbecued Peppers and Aubergine, 192–193

    Marinated BBQ Aubergine with Bowtie Pasta, 131

    Mixed Greens with Barbecued Summer Vegetables and Blue Cheese, 77

    Pasta Salad with Barbecued Vegetables and Garlic-Chipotle Dressing, 88–89

    pizza with BBQ aubergine, Garlic, and Mozzarella, 112

Aussie Chips with Sweet Chili Sauce, 100

avocados

    Corn, Black Bean, and Avocado Salad, 86

    Guacamole, 48

    Pear and Avocado Salsa, 39

B

baking stones, 12

balsamic vinegar, 214

Bananas with Ice Cream and Chocolate, Barbecued, 210

barbecue baskets, 12

barbecuing techniques, 13–15, 16

    See also cooking techniques

barbecues

    choosing, 11

    gas, 11

    indoor, 15–16

    preheating, 13–14

    tools for, 12

Basil Pesto, 23

Basil-Pesto Stuffed Mushrooms, 60

basmati rice, 214

    See also rice

BBQ Sauce, Fresh, 31

beans

    Black Bean and Cheese Burritos, 180

    Black Bean Sauce, 32

    Cannellini Bean Spread with Barbecued Red Pepper, 71

    Corn, Black Bean, and Avocado Salad, 86

    dried, 17–18

    Fajitas with barbecued squash, Refried Beans, and Fresh Squash Blossoms, 175

    Refried Bean Burritos with Smoked Gouda and Spicy Tomato Sauce, 183

    Tacos with BBQ Peppers, Black Beans, and Blue Cheese, 176

Beets and Goats Cheese, Red Lettuce Salad with Barbecued, 79

berries. *See* specific types

black beans

    Black Bean and Cheese Burritos, 180

    Black Bean Sauce, 32

    Corn, Black Bean, and Avocado Salad, 86

fermented, 215
Tacos with BBQ Peppers, Black Beans, and Blue
Cheese, 176
blanching, 17
blue cheese
Iceberg Lettuce with Barbecued Figs and Creamy Blue
Cheese Dressing, 84
Purple Figs Stuffed with Blue Cheese, 57
Tacos with BBQ Peppers, Black Beans, and Blue
Cheese, 176
blueberries
Fresh Blueberry Sauce, 33
Peach and Blueberry Salsa, 36
bok choy, 214
Baby Bok Choy with Lemon Miso Sauce, 92
Barbecued Bok Choy with Green Curry Rice, 139
Boysenberry Sauce, 33
Brie and Mango Quesadillas, 186
Broccoli and Mushrooms en Papillote with Paprika, Feta, and
Dill Seed, 122
broccoli rabe, 214
Polenta with Broccoli Rabe and Portobello
Mushrooms, 149
Bruschetta, 67
bulgur wheat, 214
burgers
Barbecued Tempeh Burgers, 202
Tofu Burgers, 203
burritos, 171
Barbecued Vegetables and Rice Burritos, 182
Black Bean and Cheese Burritos, 180
Burritos with Spinach, Artichokes, Barbecued Red Bell
Pepper, and Feta Cheese, 184
Refried Bean Burritos with Smoked Gouda and Spicy
Tomato Sauce, 18

C

cabbage
Barbecued Vegetables and Rice Burritos, 182
Caesar Salad with Smoky Barbecued Tofu, 83
cannellini beans, 214
Cannellini Bean Spread with Barbecued Red Pepper, 71
cantaloupe
Cantaloupe with Raspberry Sorbet, 211
Pear-Cantaloupe Salsa, 40
Carrots en Papillote, Curried Cauliflower and, 117
Cauliflower and Carrots en Papillote, Curried, 117
chapati, 214
charcoal barbecues, 11
cheese
Aubergine with Ricotta and Tomato Coulis, 59

Barbecued Cheese Sandwiches with Cremini
Mushrooms, 201
Barbecued Corn and Cheddar Cheese Polenta, 151
Barbecued Portobello Mushrooms with Couscous and
Gruyère Cheese, 136
Barbecued Bartlett Pears with Savoury Ricotta
Cheese, 208
Barbecued Spinach Rolls Stuffed with Tofu and Feta, 58
Barbecued Tomatillos with Potato Tacos and
Cheese, 179
Barbecued Tomato and Cheese Sandwiches, 194
BBQ Onions and Courgettes with Gorgonzola
Polenta, 150
Black Beans and Jack Cheese Burritos, 180
Brie and Mango Quesadillas, 186
Broccoli and Mushrooms en Papillote with Paprika,
Feta, and Dill Seed, 122
Burritos with Spinach, Artichokes, Barbecued Red Bell
Pepper, and Feta Cheese, 184
Mushroom and Cheese Quesadillas, 185
Purple Figs Stuffed with Blue Cheese, 57
Red Lettuce Salad with Barbecued Beets and Goats
Cheese, 79
Refried Bean Burritos with Smoked Gouda and Spicy
Tomato Sauce, 183
Spinach Salad with Barbecued Peaches and Gorgonzola
Cheese, 82
Tacos with BBQ Peppers, Black Beans, and Blue
Cheese, 176
See also pizza
Cherries, Morello, 207
chickpeas
Hummus with Barbecued Garlic, 70
Chilli, Butternut Squash, and Onion Fajitas with Queso
Fresco, 174
chilli sauce, sweet, 216
chimney starters, 12
chipotle chillies, 214
chocolate
Barbecued Bananas with Ice Cream and Chocolate, 210
Barbecued Plantains with Chocolate Sauce and
Almonds, 212
BBQ Apricots with Chocolate Mousse, 207
cooking techniques, 17–19
See also barbecuing techniques
cooking terms, 16–17
corn
Barbecued Corn and Cheddar Cheese Polenta, 151
Corn, Black Bean, and Avocado Salad, 86
Corn, Potato, and Leek Fajitas, 172

Lasagna with Barbecued Corn, Kalamata Olives, and Fresh
    Tomato Sauce, 138
  Risotto with Barbecued Corn and Red Peppers, 144
  White Corn with Chili Butter, 96
courgette
  Crostini with Barbecued Courgette and Aubergine, 6
  Barbecued Vegetables and Rice Burritos, 182
  Barbecued Courgette over Mint-Pesto Risotto, 142
  BBQ Onions and Courgettes with Gorgonzola
    Polenta, 150
  BBQ Courgette, 95
  Mixed Greens with Barbecued Summer Vegetables and
    Blue Cheese, 77
  Pasta Salad with Barbecued Vegetables and Garlic-Chipotle
    Dressing, 88–89
  Pizza with Courgette, Artichokes, and Feta Cheese, 113
  Summer Squash Stuffed with Sweet Pepper Couscous *en
    Papillote*, 122
  Summer Squashes with Lemon Basil, 93
  Courgette, Onion, and Red Bell Pepper Skewers, 158
couscous, 214
  Barbecued Portobello Mushrooms with Couscous and
    Gruyère Cheese, 136
  Summer Squash Stuffed with Sweet Pepper Couscous
    en Papillote, 122
crema, 214
crème fraîche, 214
crostini, 214
  Crostini with Fresh Tomatoes, Basil, and Garlic, 65
  Crostini with Barbecued Courgette and Aubergine, 66
Cumin and Coriander Seed-Encrusted Tofu, 169

D

desserts
  Barbecued Bananas with Ice Cream and Chocolate, 210
  Barbecued Morello Cherries, 207
  Barbecued Pineapple with Balsamic Vinegar and Brown
    Sugar, 213
  Barbecued Plantains with Chocolate Sauce and
    Almonds, 212
  Barbecued Bartlett Pears with Savoury Ricotta
    Cheese, 208
  Bartlett Pears with Butterscotch Sauce, 211
  BBQ Apricots with Chocolate Mousse, 207
  Cantaloupe with Frozen Yogurt, 211
  Nectarines with Almond Glaze, 208
  Strawberries Soaked in Late-Harvest Riesling, 206
  Yellow Peaches with Ginger Glaze, 209
Dilled Yogurt and Sour Cream Sauce, 51
dipping sauces. *See* sauces

dips and spreads
  Barbecued Red Bell Pepper Mayonnaise, 47
  BBQ Aubergine Spread, 72
  Cannellini Bean Spread with Barbecued Red Pepper, 71
  Garlic-Herb Mayonnaise, 46
  Garlic Jam, 68
  Guacamole, 48
  Hummus with Barbecued Garlic, 70
  See also salsas

E

electric barbecues, 15
endive, 215
  BBQ Endive Salad with Golden Raisins, 76
  Sweet Rolls with Barbecued Peppers and Endive, 198

F

fajitas, 170
  Chilli, Butternut Squash, and Onion Fajitas with Queso
    Fresco, 174
  Corn, Potato, and Leek Fajitas, 172
  Fajitas with barbecued squash, Refried Beans, and Fresh
    Squash Blossoms, 175
fennel
  Pasta with Barbecued Fennel and Asparagus, 137
  Saffron Rice with Barbecued Fennel, Asparagus, and
    Leeks, 141
feta cheese
  Barbecued Spinach Rolls Stuffed with Tofu and Feta, 58
  Broccoli and Mushrooms *en Papillote* with Paprika,
    Feta, and Dill Seed, 122
  Burritos with Spinach, Artichokes, Barbecued Red Bell
    Pepper, and Feta Cheese, 184
  Individual Pizzas with Tomatoes, Feta, and Kalamata
    Olives, 115
  Pizza with Courgette, Artichokes, and Feta Cheese, 113
Fettuccine with Barbecued Sweet-Potato Puree, 133
figs
  Iceberg Lettuce with Barbecued Figs and Creamy Blue
    Cheese Dressing, 84
  Purple Figs Stuffed with Blue Cheese, 57
Focaccia with Barbecued Portobello Mushrooms, 195
fruits
  dried, 19
  See also specific types
Fusilli Pasta in Caper Cream Sauce with Barbecued Aubergine
and Red Pepper Strips, 130

G

garlic, 215
  Garlic-Herb Mayonnaise, 46
  Garlic Jam, 68
  Garlic-Soy Marinade, 29

gas barbecues, 11

grains

    cooking, 18

    See also couscous; rice

Greaseproof paper, 215

Guacamole, 48

H

Hearts of Palm, Fresh Greens with Barbecued, 78

Honey-Ginger Marinade, 27

hors d'oeuvres

    Aubergine with Ricotta and Tomato Coulis, 59

    Barbecued Artichokes with Lemon Butter and Summer Savoury, 63

    Barbecued Kalamata Olives, 61

    Barbecued Pita Triangles, 69

    Barbecued Spinach Rolls Stuffed with Tofu and Feta, 58

    Basil-Pesto Stuffed Mushrooms, 60

    Bruschetta, 67

    Crostini with Fresh Tomatoes, Basil, and Garlic, 65

    Crostini with Barbecued Courgette and Aubergine, 66

    Jícama and Barbecued Bell Peppers, 73

    Lettuce Wraps with Barbecued Red Peppers and Kalamata Olives, 56

    Mushrooms Stuffed with Couscous, Mint Pesto, and Walnuts, 62

    Purple Figs Stuffed with Blue Cheese, 57

    See also dips and spreads

Horseradish Sauce, Creamy, 53

Hummus with Barbecued Garlic, 70

I

Iceberg Lettuce with Barbecued Figs and Creamy Blue Cheese Dressing, 84

indirect barbecuing, 13

indoor barbecues, 15–16

ingredients, measuring, 18–19

J

jalapeños

    pickled, 215

    See also peppers

jícama, 215

    Jícama and Barbecued Bell Peppers, 73

    Jícama and Mango Salsa with Jalapeños, 43

K

kalamata olives, 215

    See also olives

kebabs. *See* skewered entrées

L

Lasagna with Barbecued Corn, Kalamata Olives, and Fresh Tomato Sauce, 138

Lavash with Barbecued Peppers and Aubergine, 192–193

leeks

    Corn, Potato, and Leek Fajitas, 172

    Saffron Rice with Barbecued Fennel, Asparagus, and Leeks, 141

lemon grass, 215

Lettuce Wraps with Barbecued Red Peppers and Kalamata Olives, 56

M

mangos

    Brie and Mango Quesadillas, 186

    Jícama and Mango Salsa with Jalapeños, 43

    Mango and Papaya Salsa with Jalapeños, 37

marinades

    Garlic-Soy Marinade, 29

    Honey-Ginger Marinade, 27

    Raspberry Vinegar Marinade, 28

    Soy and Balsamic Fusion Marinade, 26

    Spicy Plum Sauce Marinade, 30

mayonnaise

    Barbecued Red Bell Pepper Mayonnaise, 47

    Garlic-Herb Mayonnaise, 46

measurements, 18–19

melon

    Cantaloupe with Raspberry Sorbet, 211

    Pear-Cantaloupe Salsa, 40

Mexican Crema, 48

Mint Pesto, 23

mirin, 215

miso, 215

mushrooms

    Asparagus and Mushroom Pizza with Mustard, Dill, Mozzarella, and Feta, 109

    Asparagus, Shiitake Mushrooms, and Tofu *en Papillote*, 119

    Barbecued Cheese Sandwiches with Cremini Mushrooms, 201

    Barbecued Portobello Mushrooms with Couscous and Gruyère Cheese, 136

    Basil-Pesto Stuffed Mushrooms, 60

    Broccoli and Mushrooms *en Papillote* with Paprika, Feta, and Dill Seed, 122

    Focaccia with Barbecued Portobello Mushrooms, 195

    Mushroom and Cheese Quesadillas, 185

    Mushrooms Stuffed with Couscous, Mint Pesto, and Walnuts, 62

    Pasta with BBQ Artichokes and Fresh Shiitake Mushrooms, 134–135

    Polenta with Broccoli Rabe and Portobello Mushrooms, 149

Portobello Mushrooms in Mustard Marinade over Green Risotto, 146

Potatoes, Mushrooms, and Shallots *en Papillote*, 118

Red Potato and Mushroom Skewers, 160

Tempeh, Mushroom, and Cherry Tomato Skewers, 165

N

Nectarines with Almond Glaze, 208

nopales, 215

Nopalito and Tomato Quesadillas, 187

nuts and seeds, toasting, 19

O

olives

Barbecued Kalamata Olives, 61

Individual Pizzas with Tomatoes, Feta, and Kalamata Olives, 115

Lasagna with Barbecued Corn, Kalamata Olives, and Fresh Tomato Sauce, 138

Lettuce Wraps with Barbecued Red Peppers and Kalamata Olives, 56

onions

Barbecued Onions with Red Wine Vinaigrette, 95

BBQ Onions and Courgettes with Gorgonzola Polenta, 150

Chilli, Butternut Squash, and Onion Fajitas with Queso Fresco, 174

Courgette, Onion, and Red Bell Pepper Skewers, 158

Pasta with BBQ Asparagus and Onions, 127

P

Papaya Salsa with Jalapeños, Mango and, 37

papillote packets

Asparagus, Shiitake Mushrooms, and Tofu *en Papillote*, 119

Broccoli and Mushrooms *en Papillote* with Paprika, Feta, and Dill Seed, 122

Curried Cauliflower and Carrots *en Papillote*, 117

instructions for, 104

Potatoes, Mushrooms, and Shallots *en Papillote*, 118

Summer Squash Stuffed with Sweet Pepper Couscous *en Papillote*, 122

Summer Squashes *en Papillote* with Tex-Mex Seasonings, 120

pasta

cooking, 124

Fettuccine with Barbecued Sweet-Potato Puree, 133

Fusilli Pasta in Caper Cream Sauce with Barbecued Aubergine and Red Pepper Strips, 130

Lasagna with Barbecued Corn, Kalamata Olives, and Fresh Tomato Sauce, 138

Marinated BBQ Aubergine with Bowtie Pasta, 131

Pasta Salad with Barbecued Radicchio and Sweet Peppers, 87

Pasta Salad with Barbecued Vegetables and Garlic-Chipotle Dressing, 88–89

Pasta with BBQ Artichokes and Fresh Shiitake Mushrooms, 134–135

Pasta with BBQ Asparagus and Onions, 127

Pasta with Barbecued Fennel and Asparagus, 137

Vermicelli with Barbecued Tomato Sauce, 128

peaches

Peach and Blueberry Salsa, 36

Peach and Pineapple Salsa with Fresh Tarragon, 42

Spinach Salad with Barbecued Peaches and Gorgonzola Cheese, 82

Yellow Peaches with Ginger Glaze, 209

peanuts

Peanut Sauce, 46

Spicy Peanut Tofu Skewers with a Trio of Bell Peppers, 164

pears

Barbecued Bartlett Pears with Savoury Ricotta Cheese, 208

Bartlett Pears with Butterscotch Sauce, 211

Pear and Avocado Salsa, 39

Pear-Cantaloupe Salsa, 40

peppers

Barbecued Red Bell Pepper Mayonnaise, 47

Barbecued Vegetables and Rice Burritos, 182

BBQ Pepper and Chard Pizza with Cumin, Jalapeños, and Coriander, 114

Burritos with Spinach, Artichokes, Barbecued Red Bell Pepper, and Feta Cheese, 184

Cannellini Bean Spread with Barbecued Red Pepper, 71

Courgette, Onion, and Red Bell Pepper Skewers, 158

Fusilli Pasta in Caper Cream Sauce with Barbecued Aubergine and Red Pepper Strips, 130

Japanese Aubergine and Red Bell Pepper Sandwich with Pesto, 197

Jícama and Barbecued Bell Peppers, 73

Lavash with Barbecued Peppers and Aubergine, 192–193

Lettuce Wraps with Barbecued Red Peppers and Kalamata Olives, 56

Pasta Salad with Barbecued Radicchio and Sweet Peppers, 87

Risotto with Barbecued Corn and Red Peppers, 144

Soft Tacos with Barbecued Tofu and Pickled Jalapeños, 178

Spicy Peanut Tofu Skewers with a Trio of Bell Peppers, 164

Spinach Salad with Spiced Walnuts and Fire-Roasted Red Bell Pepper, 80

Sweet Rolls with Barbecued Peppers and Endive, 198

Tacos with BBQ Peppers, Black Beans, and Blue Cheese, 176

pesto
  Barbecued Courgette over Mint-Pesto Risotto, 142
  Basil Pesto, 23
  Basil-Pesto Stuffed Mushrooms, 60
  Japanese Aubergine and Red Bell Pepper Sandwich with
      Pesto, 197
  Mint Pesto, 23
  Pesto Pizza, 107
pineapples
  Barbecued Pineapple with Balsamic Vinegar and Brown
      Sugar, 213
  Peach and Pineapple Salsa with Fresh Tarragon, 42
  Tempeh, Pineapple, and Jalapeño Skewers, 157
Pistachio-Encrusted Tofu with Basmati Rice, 143
Pita Triangles, Barbecued, 69
pizza
  Asparagus and Mushroom Pizza with Mustard, Dill,
      Mozzarella, and Feta, 109
  Asparagus Pizza, 108
  Basic Pizza Crust, 105–106
    Individual Pizzas with Tomatoes, Feta, and Kalamata
        Olives, 115
  BBQ Pepper and Chard Pizza with Cumin, Jalapeños,
      and Coriander, 114
  Pesto Pizza, 107
  Pizza with Garlic Tomato Sauce, Ricotta, and Fresh
      Greens, 111
  pizza with BBQ aubergine, Garlic, and
      Mozzarella, 112
  Pizza with Courgette, Artichokes, and Feta Cheese, 113
Plantains with Chocolate Sauce and Almonds, Barbecued, 212
Plum Sauce Marinade, Spicy, 30
polenta, 215
  Barbecued Corn and Cheddar Cheese Polenta, 151
  Barbecued Polenta with Tomato Coulis, 147
  cooking, 125
  BBQ Aubergine Parmesan with Soft Polenta, 152
  BBQ Onions and Courgettes with Gorgonzola
      Polenta, 150
  Polenta with Broccoli Rabe and Portobello
      Mushrooms, 149
ponzu sauce, 215
  Creamy Ponzu Sauce, 52
portobello mushrooms, 215
  Barbecued Portobello Mushrooms with Couscous and
      Gruyère Cheese, 136
  Focaccia with Barbecued Portobello Mushrooms, 195
  Polenta with Broccoli Rabe and Portobello
      Mushrooms, 149
  Portobello Mushrooms in Mustard Marinade over Green
      Risotto, 146

potatoes
  Aussie Chips with Sweet Chili Sauce, 100
  Barbecued Red Potatoes, 98
  Barbecued Tomatillos with Potato Tacos and Cheese, 179
  Corn, Potato, and Leek Fajitas, 172
  Potatoes, Mushrooms, and Shallots en Papillote, 118
  Red Potato and Mushroom Skewers, 160
  Russet Potato Wedges, 101
Q
quesadillas, 171
  Brie and Mango Quesadillas, 186
  Mushroom and Cheese Quesadillas, 185
  Nopalito and Tomato Quesadillas, 187
queso fresca, 216
R
radicchio, 216
  Pasta Salad with Barbecued Radicchio and Sweet
      Peppers, 87
Raspberry Sorbet, Cantaloupe with, 209
Raspberry Vinegar Marinade, 28
Red Lettuce Salad with Barbecued Beets and Goats Cheese, 79
red peppers. See peppers
Remoulade Sauce, 53
rice
  Arborio, 125, 214
  Barbecued Bok Choy with Green Curry Rice, 139
  Barbecued Vegetables and Rice Burritos, 182
  Barbecued Courgette over Mint-Pesto Risotto, 142
  Basmati Rice with Barbecued Summer Squashes, 140
  cooking, 124–125
  Pistachio-Encrusted Tofu with Basmati Rice, 143
  Portobello Mushrooms in Mustard Marinade over Green
      Risotto, 146
  Risotto with Barbecued Corn and Red Peppers, 144
  Saffron Rice with Barbecued Fennel, Asparagus, and
      Leeks, 141
  rice wine vinegar, 216
risotto. See rice
Rolls with Barbecued Peppers and Endive, Sweet, 198
S
Saffron Rice with Barbecued Fennel, Asparagus, and Leeks,
141
salads
  BBQ Endive Salad with Golden Raisins, 76
  Barbecued Tomato Salad with Fresh Mozzarella Cheese, 85
  Caesar Salad with Smoky Barbecued Tofu, 83
  Corn, Black Bean, and Avocado Salad, 86
  Fresh Greens with Barbecued Hearts of Palm, 78

Iceberg Lettuce with Barbecued Figs and Creamy Blue
    Cheese Dressing, 84
Mixed Greens with Barbecued Summer Vegetables and
    Blue Cheese, 77
Pasta Salad with Barbecued Radicchio and Sweet Peppers, 87
Pasta Salad with Barbecued Vegetables and Garlic-Chipotle
    Dressing, 88–89
Red Lettuce Salad with Barbecued Beets and
    Goats Cheese, 79
Spinach Salad with Barbecued Peaches and Gorgonzola
    Cheese, 82
Spinach Salad with Spiced Walnuts and Fire-Roasted
    Red Bell Pepper, 80
salsas
    Jícama and Mango Salsa with Jalapeños, 43
    Mango and Papaya Salsa with Jalapeños, 37
    Peach and Blueberry Salsa, 36
    Peach and Pineapple Salsa with Fresh Tarragon, 42
    Pear and Avocado Salsa, 39
    Pear-Cantaloupe Salsa, 40
    Salsa Fresca, 45
    Smooth Tomatillo Salsa, 38
sandwiches
    Barbecued Artichoke Panini, 194
    Barbecued Cheese Sandwiches with Cremini
        Mushrooms, 201
    Barbecued Tomato and Cheese Sandwiches, 194
    BBQ Aubergine on Focaccia, 196
    Focaccia with Barbecued Portobello Mushrooms, 195
    Japanese Aubergine and Red Bell Pepper Sandwich with
        Pesto, 197
    Sweet Rolls with Barbecued Peppers and Endive, 198
    Tofu 'BLT' Sandwich, 200
    See also burgers; wraps
sauces
    Basil Pesto, 23
    Black Bean Sauce, 32
    Boysenberry Sauce, 33
    Creamy Horseradish Sauce, 53
    Creamy Ponzu Sauce, 52
    Dilled Yogurt and Sour Cream Sauce, 51
    Fresh BBQ Sauce, 31
    Fresh Blueberry Sauce, 33
    Mexican Crema, 48
    Mint Pesto, 23
    Peanut Sauce, 46
    Remoulade Sauce, 53
    Spicy Tahini Sauce, 50
    Tomato Coulis, 24
    See also salsas

seeds. See nuts and seeds
sesame tahini, 216
shiitake mushrooms, 216
    Asparagus, Shiitake Mushrooms, and Tofu
        en Papillote, 119
    Pasta with BBQ Artichokes and Fresh Shiitake
        Mushrooms, 134–135
shish kebabs. See skewered entrées
side dishes
    Asparagus with Watercress Sauce, 90
    Aussie Chips with Sweet Chili Sauce, 100
    Baby Bok Choy with Lemon Miso Sauce, 92
    Barbecued Onions with Red Wine Vinaigrette, 95
    Barbecued Red Potatoes, 98
    Barbecued Sweet Potatoes, 99
    BBQ Courgette, 95
    Russet Potato Wedges, 101
    Summer Squashes with Lemon Basil, 93
    White Corn with Chilli Butter, 96
skewered entrées
    Courgette, Onion, and Red Bell Pepper Skewers, 158
    Cumin and Coriander Seed-Encrusted Tofu, 169
    Curry-Marinated Tofu Skewers with Jalapeño and Lime, 161
    Red Potato and Mushroom Skewers, 160
    Skewered Tofu and Tomatoes, 163
    Spicy Peanut Tofu Skewers with a Trio of Bell Peppers, 164
    Tempeh, Mushroom, and Cherry Tomato Skewers, 165
    Tempeh, Pineapple, and Jalapeño Skewers, 157
    Tofu in Garlic-Soy Marinade, 168
    Tofu Sates, 167
smoker boxes, 12
soba, 216
Soy and Balsamic Fusion Marinade, 26
spinach
    Burritos with Spinach, Artichokes, Barbecued Red Bell
Pepper, and Feta Cheese, 184
    Barbecued Spinach Rolls Stuffed with Tofu and Feta, 58
    Spinach Salad with Barbecued Peaches and Gorgonzola
        Cheese, 82
    Spinach Salad with Spiced Walnuts and Fire-Roasted Red
        Bell Pepper, 80
spreads. See dips and spreads
squash
    Basmati Rice with Barbecued Summer Squashes, 140
    Chilli, Butternut Squash, and Onion Fajitas with Queso
        Fresco, 174
    Fajitas with Barbecued Squash, Refried Beans,
    and Fresh Squash Blossoms, 175
    Summer Squash Stuffed with Sweet Pepper Couscous
        en Papillote, 123

Summer Squashes *en Papillote* with Tex-Mex
    Seasonings, 120
Summer Squashes with Lemon Basil, 93
Stock, Vegetable, 25
Strawberries Soaked in Late-Harvest Riesling, 206
summer squash. *See* squash
sweet chilli sauce, 216
sweet potatoes
    Barbecued Sweet Potatoes, 99
    Fettuccine with Barbecued Sweet-Potato Puree, 133
Sweet Rolls with Barbecued Peppers and Endive, 198
Swiss chard
    BBQ Pepper and Chard Pizza with Cumin, Jalapeños,
        and Coriander, 114

T

tacos, 171
    Barbecued Tomatillos with Potato Tacos and
        Cheese, 179
    Soft Tacos with Barbecued Tofu and Pickled Jalapeños, 178
    Tacos with BBQ Peppers, Black Beans, and Blue
        Cheese, 176
Tahini Sauce, Spicy, 50
tempeh, 216
    Barbecued Tempeh Burgers, 202
    Tempeh, Mushroom, and Cherry Tomato Skewers, 165
    Tempeh, Pineapple, and Jalapeño Skewers, 157
tofu, 216
    Anaheim Chilli and Curry Tofu Wrap, 191
    Asparagus, Shiitake Mushrooms, and Tofu *en Papillote*, 119
    Barbecued Spinach Rolls Stuffed with Tofu and Feta, 58
    Caesar Salad with Smoky Barbecued Tofu, 83
    Cumin and Coriander Seed-Encrusted Tofu, 169
    Curry-Marinated Tofu Skewers with Jalapeño and Lime, 161
        Pistachio-Encrusted Tofu with Basmati Rice, 143
    Skewered Tofu and Tomatoes, 163
    Soft Tacos with Barbecued Tofu and Pickled Jalapeños, 178
    Spicy Peanut Tofu Skewers with a Trio of Bell Peppers, 164
    Tofu 'BLT' Sandwich, 200
    Tofu Burgers, 203
    Tofu in Garlic-Soy Marinade, 168
    Tofu Sates, 167

tomatillos, 216
    Barbecued Tomatillos with Potato Tacos and Cheese, 179
    Smooth Tomatillo Salsa, 38
tomatoes
    Barbecued Polenta with Tomato Coulis, 147
    Barbecued Tomato and Cheese Sandwiches, 194
    Barbecued Tomato Salad with Fresh Mozzarella Cheese, 85
    dried, 214
    Nopalito and Tomato Quesadillas, 187
    Salsa Fresca, 45
    Skewered Tofu and Tomatoes, 163
    Tempeh, Mushroom, and Cherry Tomato Skewers, 165
    Tomato Coulis, 24
    Vermicelli with Barbecued Tomato Sauce, 128
tools, 12

V

vegetables. *See also* specific types
    Barbecued Vegetables and Rice Burritos, 182
    dried, 19
    Mixed Greens with Barbecued Summer Vegetables and
        Blue Cheese, 77
    steaming, 19
Vegetable Stock, 25
Vermicelli with Barbecued Tomato Sauce, 128

W

walnuts
    Mushrooms Stuffed with Couscous, Mint Pesto, and
        Walnuts, 62
    Spinach Salad with Spiced Walnuts and Fire-Roasted Red
        Bell Pepper, 80
wasabi, 216
Watercress Sauce, Asparagus with, 90
wraps
    Anaheim Chilli and Curry Tofu Wrap, 191
    Lavash with Barbecued Peppers and Aubergine, 192–193

Y

yogurt
    Cantaloupe with Frozen Yogurt, 211
    Dilled Yogurt and Sour Cream Sauce, 51

Z